Flights of Fancy, Souls of Grace

Flights of Fancy, Souls of Grace

More True Tales from Extraordinary Lives

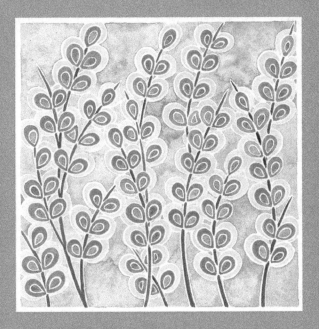

RICHIE DAVIS

Forty Years of Writing from *The Recorder*
of Western Massachusetts

Haley's

Athol, Massachusetts

Stories first appeared between 1982 and 2021 in the *Recorder* of Greenfield, Massachusetts, and are used by permission of Newspapers of Massachusetts, Inc.

Proof read by Richard Bruno

Cover art *First Signs of Spring* in watercolor on paper by Ami Fagin

Cover design by Robin Locke Monda

Author photo on back cover by Lindy Whiton

Haley's
488 South Main Street
Athol, MA 01331

International Standard Book Number 978-1-948380-82-9,
        trade paperback
International Standard Book Number 978-1-948380-83-6,
        ebook, watermarked pdf

Library of Congress cataloguing in publishing pending

In memory of
Paula, for her work building hope and empathy,
Irmarie, for her boundless humanity,
Alan, for his loving compassion and embrace of a global family

Contents

Uncovering Hidden Magic

a foreword by Pat Ryan and Tim Hilchey

When we returned to Franklin County from New York City after more than thirty years away, it was not surprising that we found ourselves rediscovering this special corner of the world. Iridescent sunsets and bird trills provide daily reminders of just how special this corner is.

But in a touch of serendipity, dormant friendships have also been rekindled. And so we find ourselves writing about the life's work of our friend and colleague Richie Davis, who long ago "rediscovered" his home here in Franklin County.

It seems preordained that Richie landed here in 1976 in a place that the Massachusetts Office of Travel and Tourism has branded "a hidden gem." It proved to be his ideal neck of the woods, and he hewed his unique newspaper trail in these old-growth villages and towns. His beat was designated by various names, from West County reporter to county editor and later to staff writer, covering alternative energy and innovative agriculture.

None of these titles boxed him in. They don't begin to explain the way he unearthed his characters or the satisfaction he gained by writing about them. Some were newly arrived; others had been around for generations (and damn proud of it); some people—us included—had left only to be lured back later. But each Richie Davis byline illustrates an essential element of what makes him the special storyteller he is: an uncanny ability to uncover the magic hidden in everyday existence.

The county—twenty-six towns and cities covering about seven hundred square miles of western Massachusetts — is the most rural in the state, but hardly the sticks. The inhabitants have a wide assortment of occupations and avocations. Richie gave voice to artisans like Wang Hui-Ming, an eighty-two-year-old calligrapher-artist-poet at home in Montague Center, and Ted Renaud, 63, who, though completely deaf, became a zealous contra dancer at Greenfield's Guiding Star Grange Hall.

Richie wrote through the divisive 2016 election and then, post-retirement, during the frightening 2019-2022 COVID pandemic lockdowns. He interviewed activists as noteworthy as Randy Kehler, advocate for social justice and inspiration for Daniel Ellsberg's release of the Pentagon Papers, and Paula Green, a global peacemaker and founding director of the Karuna Center for Peacebuilding. He wrote features about an exchange among residents of Leverett and a rural county in eastern Kentucky and about a gathering of townspeople who have been singing together on the Montague Town Common every single day since COVID lockdowns began.

The columns in this book, his third collection, are about people and places like these and were published in the *Recorder*—a daily newspaper must be of a piece with its county—from 1982 to the present.

We worked at the *Recorder* with Richie back in the halcyon days of the 1980s when Irmarie Jones, Bob Laramie, and Denny Wilkins were among the bright lights on the staff.

Though halcyon, the days were never tranquil: police radios quacked with reports of fires and accidents while typewriters and teletypes clacked. At the back of the room, paste-up artists laid out the strips of copy and carried the finished pages down to the basement. When the presses below rumbled to life, it was the signal that it was OK to relax for a while.

The *Recorder* was a place where locals sometimes walked through the front door on Hope Street right into the newsroom to share their thoughts with us. There were scoops, frustration, overtime, and not a few long nights followed by morning hangovers. Pat interviewed the poets Richard Wilbur in Cummington and Adrienne Rich in Montague. Tim wrote about two kid sisters who were fiddle virtuosos and events like a fiery train derailment and the epic Marvin Hagler-Tommy Hearns boxing match.

Nostalgia warning: amid it all, we were family. We made lasting friendships.

Was it fate or luck that brought us together in the *Recorder* newsroom at the same time? Whatever it was, we learned a lot from each other, especially how to translate into newsprint the voices we heard everywhere around us—on the street, in town meetings, diners and bars, and at elections, protests, fairs, concerts, and clubs. For some, it was the first exposure to journalism.

The advantage of a small newsroom of twenty or so reporters and editors was the mix. We weren't separated into cubicles. The *Recorder* was an afternoon paper then, hitting the streets about noon. I, Pat, yelled "Stop the presses!" on the phone to the printers on the morning of the Challenger disaster. We shared tips and wrote and/or edited articles for the business, food, home, entertainment, real estate, seniors, and religion pages.

For a brief time, Richie migrated to become "Weekend" editor at the *Springfield Daily News*, before returning to his beloved *Recorder*, capping a forty-plus-year career. We also left the *Recorder* for bigger pasture—the Worcester *Telegram*, the *New York Times,* the *International Herald-Tribune* in Paris, ending our journalism careers at the *Times*.

At these bigger newspapers, we worked alongside scores of talented reporters, photographers, and editors. We forged friendships around the world. And yet, overall, we don't recall anyone saying they had as many adventures as Richie Davis did while on the job. He knew a place with character when he discovered it.

❖ ❖ ❖

Pat Ryan and Tim Hilchey are retired *New York Times* journalists who worked at the Greenfield *Recorder* in the 1980s.

Revisiting Flights of Fancy

an introduction by Richie Davis

I couldn't have imagined before retiring a few years back that many of the feature articles I'd written over forty-plus years would morph into three volumes of collected stories as they have, just as I'd never conceived of spending more than a couple of years working in that Greenfield, Massachusetts, newsroom.

This third collection in itself seemed improbable once the ordeals of re-editing, promoting, and marketing my two first two books — during a pandemic, no less—became clear to me.

"No way," I said.

"Well, probably not."

"OK, maybe."

Once I considered all the stories I'd been unable to include first in *Inner Landscapes* and then in *Good Will & Ice Cream*, expanding my collection of collections to three volumes seemed a charm: a well-rounded, satisfying trilogy.

Sharing the stories anew at readings and connecting with enthusiastic audiences became a delightful surprise for me. And then

1

having my habitual reporter's role turned on its head for interviews felt like an odd role reversal. The question I've been asked most often—"How did you happen to pick these stories?"—will no doubt come back to haunt me with this third volume.

These articles, written between a few years following my 1976 arrival at the newspaper and beyond my 2019 retirement, shouldn't be at all construed as runners-up or less deserving than those in the first book, which I imagined to be principally profiles, or the second, which I expanded to encompass a broader array of features. I'd hoped to include some of these stories in those earlier books. but they got away from me. My roundup went awry.

❖ ❖ ❖

There's something both tremendously unnerving and deeply satisfying about writing and editing for a newspaper, day in and day out, for four-plus decades—especially since no two days are exactly alike, and you never know what feats you'll be called to dive into from one day—or even one minute—to the next.

Especially at a small newspaper with its tiny staff, the radio scanner might sound with a fire just as you're about to walk out the door at the end of a long day, or maybe it's a car crash on the opposite end of the county that you're sent off to on a snowy afternoon when you've been struggling with an intricate, controversial story. Or someone drops a bombshell revelation in the middle of a meeting that dramatically changes the story you expected to be banging out on your keyboard immediately afterward.

No wonder our publisher referred to our newspaper as "the daily miracle," completely remade each day. And that was before reporters were expected sometimes to write and update stories during a meeting while also taking photos and shooting videos for added content.

My beats—the coverage zones assigned to me—varied over time, including nine western hill towns, the courts, state and regional government, politics, energy and the environment, and finally a mix of those regional issues so that when occasionally asked to describe my turf, I'd simply tell people, "I cover the waterfront."

It's a terrain that's always felt like my true home, as I told a chamber of commerce gathering as I was about to retire:

Franklin County is all-natural, down-home New England, where real-life stories abound.

There's nothing pompous or concocted about this neck of the woods. If I've had a bias in my reporting all these years, it's that the soul of this place just resonates so deeply for me. It's a breath of fresh air where quality of life, rather than quantity of life, truly matters.

Given the array of news stories that are usually popping, even in a seemingly mundane, semi-rural area like ours in western Massachusetts, you might well wonder how it is that a reporter on a small paper can get to write stories that are so far removed from the "hard news" realm—like about the circuitous "mail trail" of a letter between neighboring towns or my series of stories about the burgeoning popularity of yogurt and its effect on our region.

Chalk that up to luck or to the blessing of having worked for editors who saw the value of running a few stories now and then from far off the beaten path.

From my perch in our nearly windowless newsroom, to relieve myself from the requisite cops-'n'-robbers reporting and following statehouse antics, I relished any chance to soar with flights of fancy stories. Some of those were sparked by wonder about, say, life on the boundary between time zones or imagining a tour of not-so-distant attractions like the childhood home of Dr. Seuss or of Mary of "little lamb" fame.

Among my most memorable flights was the fantastic three-year-long, dust-to-dessert adventure covering Denise DiPaolo as she created her destination restaurant in what had been a vacant, dilapidated former laundromat that she bought for one dollar from the town.

Yes, at times I was tied down covering our rep in Congress, two neighborhood nuke plants, and budget wrangling. But simply getting to write about fascinating, imaginative characters like sculptor Tim de Christopher, spirited tire salesman Len Weeks, or scissors-wielding sheep shearer Kevin Ford was for me an opportunity to fly off with nearly fantasical subjects.

It's the stories about living heroes in our midst that helps bind community together, I found. Seeking out those characters, listening carefully to their stories and spinning them into readable prose can create a more cohesive, connected community. That's one aspect of my work that I relished.

It's that sense of community connections that made my anything-but-routine pounding of the beat for *The Daily Grind* so satisfying and meaningful. Former co-workers Pat Ryan and Tim Hilchey said they couldn't recall any reporter or editor they'd met who'd had as many on-the-job larks as I did. So maybe I was doing something right after all.

This reporter treasured all of those flights of fancy, and all the souls of grace I got to share with readers. I hope you'll savor them, too.

A seven-headed serpent protects the Buddha at the Cambodian Temple, Leverett, Massachusetts

Compassion's Glow

November 19, 2005

My intrigue over the Cambodian temple just up the hill from where I live arose after visits to its closest neighbor, the much more prominent Japanese Peace Pagoda that was the first of its kind in North America, built in 1985. My introduction to the Cambodian monks who lived there resulted in volunteering to drive three saffron-robed clergy to daily English lessons twenty miles away over the following year. The lively car-ride conversations might well someday become a story of their own.

🏵 🏵 🏵

There's a glow at Watkiry Vongsa Bopharam.

A pair of flickering candles on the altar of the sacred space in Leverett is dwarfed by an encased, six-foot-tall, bead-studded likeness of Cambodia's mammoth Angkor Wat temple. A majestic, saffron-cloaked Buddha oversees a dozen smaller statues of the prophet gathered from Sri Lanka, India, Japan, and elsewhere around the Buddhist world. Twin porcelain elephants hold candles waist high. Oriental rugs cover the floor of the temple, where Cambodian immigrants from around the Pioneer Valley and beyond come to pray and listen to dharma teachings.

A flick of a switch turns on a dazzling display of lights equal to those along the Franklin County Fair midway. Yet somehow the illuminated spiritual spectacle enhances the wonder of it all.

Watkiry Vongsa may seem out of place in its secluded Cave Hill setting except for the neighboring 103-foot-tall Japanese peace pagoda and temple at its peak. But tranquility envelops this 20-acre prayer center.

A brief walk along a checkerboard concrete path leads a visitor from the red-roofed temple with finials and stone lion sentries through the woods to an outdoor Buddha, his head protected from the rain by a seven-headed serpent, or naga. Further on, inside a screened pavilion decorated with colorful cloth and hanging lanterns, a plaster reclining Buddha, more than twenty feet in length, is surrounded by flowers, candles, and prayer rugs. He appears happily asleep, but Buddha is actually depicted having reached parinirvana.

Deeper in the woods and up the hill near a memorial marker for Watkiry Vongsa founding president Boay Bu and his wife is a stupa, or shrine, with the ashes of twenty or so cremated community members.

Yet the center of activity is the temple, where fragrant incense greets visitors. Its side walls are lined with images of young Buddha before enlightenment as well as those of local Cambodian families and Maha Gosananda, the world-renowned monk who founded the sanctuary. A statue of Gosananda, known as the Gandhi of Cambodia, graces a corner of the altar.

Everywhere, however, the air is bathed in a spirit of veneration and grace.

Innumerable bows, with palms pressed together, are the greetings to and from orange-robed monks, nuns, and women volunteers dressed entirely in white. Watkiry Vongsa itself means "little white flowers on the hill" and, like most flowers, the nuns and attendants abound mostly in spring and summer, when the Leverett sanctuary feels most like Cambodia itself.

In the kitchen inside one of several huts and trailers on the property, Yea Pooung and two other cooks are busy preparing the 11 a.m. morning meal for the monks from offerings brought by community members. This day in October is the end of a two-week period honoring ancestors, and offerings are particularly plentiful: fish, eggplant, roasted garlic, vegetables, and, of course, rice. The food is set out in bowls on the floor, where community members will be called to share their meal.

The monks must finish their second and final meal of the day by noon, after which they are allowed only tea and water.

Sitting cross-legged in a small bedroom in the rear of the trailer, Sovoeun Szay of Belchertown takes a few moments from preparing the meal to speak with a visitor. She's come to Leverett to care for the temple and the monks—Phorn Peap, who arrived this February directly from Cambodia, and Thong Eait, who came a year or so earlier. Neither understands much English, so both depend on volunteer tutors.

The monks, who lead prayers at 5 p.m. daily, are not burdened with preparing food, she explains. "Like kings they are."

In broken English, Szay says she comes to the Leverett temple often, sometimes for a week or more at a time. Days spent here, particularly during dharma teachings from the monks, feel to her like medicine for her soul.

❂ ❂ ❂

The shadow of a terrifying past lingers beyond the peace of the sanctuary.

Cambodia, which won independence from ninety years of French colonial rule in 1953, turned into a casualty of the war in Indochina when US forces in 1969 began bombing North Vietnamese bases there, and the country's monarchy abdicated the following year. Following years of guerrilla fighting, pro-Communist Pol Pot seized control in 1975.

His dictatorship banned religion, abolished money and private property, and moved the population from urban centers to forced labor camps. Nearly two million intellectuals, Buddhist priests, and other "enemies of the state"—roughly thirty percent of the population—died from starvation or were tortured and executed by Khmer Rouge forces during the regime, which lasted for more than

9

three years. Cambodia's 3,600 Buddhist temples were shut down, and the persecution of 60,000 clergy left only 3,000 by the time Pol Pot's regime collapsed in 1979.

"The Khmer Rouge turned Cambodia to year zero," according to the Dith Pran Holocaust Awareness Project, founded by the refugee journalist whose story was portrayed in movie *The Killing Fields*.

"They banned all institutions, including stores, banks, hospitals, schools, religion, and the family. Everyone was forced to work twelve to fourteen hours a day, every day. Children were separated from their parents to work in mobile groups or as soldiers. People were fed one watery bowl of soup with a few grains of rice thrown in.

"Babies, children, adults, and the elderly were killed everywhere. The Khmer Rouge killed people if they didn't like them, if they didn't work hard enough, if they were educated, if they came from different ethnic groups, or if they showed sympathy when their family members were taken away to be killed. It was a campaign based on instilling constant fear and keeping their victims off balance."

Thousands of Cambodian refugees immigrated to this country in the late 1970s and 1980s, many of them flocking to Massachusetts. Franklin and Hampshire counties have a combined Cambodian population of nearly five hundred, according to the 2000 census, with most of that community clustered around Amherst.

⬚ ⬚ ⬚

Inside the Leverett temple, Sovoeun and Maly Mel of Chelmsford, both dressed in white robes, sit cross-legged on the floor and recall their past. They tell of fathers, brothers, husbands, and daughters killed by the Khmer Rouge, of being uprooted from their villages, of carrying young children for days to reach the Thai border camps, and then of crowding into apartments here until they could get settled.

"My brother was a monk a long time," says Maly Mel, who arrived here in 1982. "He wouldn't take off his robes, so they shot him." Her father, daughter, and husband were all killed by Khmer Rouge.

Sovoeun recalls crossing her country on foot with her seven children to escape the Khmer Rouge after her village was blown apart and making their way toward the refugee camp in Thailand where they stayed before immigrating to the United States in 1984.

Oul Chham, a Holyoke woman who arrived in Amherst ten years ago and visits the temple frequently, sits nearby, nodding familiarly with what she hears. She remembers crossing the river with her four children, as well as her sister and brothers, to escape to Thailand.

"All the houses were burned down by Khmer Rouge. Even the temple burned down," she says, then pantomimes taking aim with a rifle. "They shoot. You don't move. They said they would rather save the bullet: it's worth more than my life. Would rather cut you with a bayonet."

Vouch An, a former rice farmer and Cambodian soldier who arrived in Amherst in 1985 with his wife and six children, remembers his ancestral village bombed by American forces searching for Vietcong in 1973 as well as houses burned by Khmer Rouge. They fled to a village in the northeast Battambang region, where most of the area's refugees hail from.

His first wife, his parents, and his youngest son died of illnesses in 1975. His second wife, Moeun Hen, saw her father die of starvation at the same time, says her daughter, Lauren Wrené Srey. All live today in Amherst.

"I didn't really have a childhood at all," says Srey, now in her thirties and speaking perfect English. She grew up in war-torn villages and refugee camps. "All I'd see was war and destruction. I had never been in a school system until I was in a camp in 1979. I didn't know another world existed with other countries, other races."

When Vouch and his family arrived in Amherst, where his cousin had settled with the sponsorship of the Lutheran church three years earlier, about fifteen Cambodian families were here. They began meeting in houses and church spaces to mark the new year and celebrate their ancestors.

"It helps us emotionally and physically to come together," explains Vouch through his stepdaughter. "We can share our common culture and understanding and we can take pride in who we are."

❈ ❈ ❈

Stories of immigrant families with members left behind in refugee camps in Thailand convinced Elaine Kenseth of Amherst to join a "mission of witness" of pastors and other lay people in 1983.

"There were seven families, and each of them had members languishing in the camps," recalls Kenseth, who repeated the trip twice more during a nine-month period and befriended Maha Gosananda, the senior surviving Cambodian monk, who had settled in Providence, Rhode Island, and was leading the pilgrimages.

"In the same way that white-steepled, Congregational churches are on the commons of very many towns in New England, the temples are in villages of Thailand and Cambodia," says Kenseth. "Here are people recovering from trauma of war and of refugee camps, and they go through resettling in a new country where everything is so different, and their spiritual leaders were not here except for this one monk."

Cave Hill's neighboring peace pagoda and temple built by the Japanese Nipponzan Myohoji Buddhist order offered a place for Cambodians to pray at first. But the refugees, visited frequently by Gosananda, sought a monk of their own and began collecting money to support one.

When twenty acres adjacent to the pagoda property became available in early 1987, Kenseth was approached by elders of the Cambodian community with two hundred dollars in hand, mounting a campaign to raise the sixty-seven thousand dollars, family by family, in a scene reminiscent of a Frank Capra movie.

"They'd say today we're going to Holyoke, to Springfield, to Amherst Crossing," she recalls. "They would all talk in Khmer, people would get their purses, and literally the money would go into a hat where everybody emptied their piggy banks."

It took ten years to build the temple and to bring the community's resident monk here, during which time a group of families started another Buddhist temple in an Amherst apartment. That temple has moved to a house in Pelham.

Kenseth says she's sometimes asked why such a small community should have two temples.

"Amherst is a town that had five Congregational churches in the fifties. People split off. That happens in organized religions."

Srey says that, while a college student, she taught Cambodian to children in the community. Young Cambodians were helped by having a Khmer students club and afterschool cultural lessons in the Amherst schools before budgets were cut several years ago. Having a way to transmit their native language and culture to young people is important, and the Pelham center attracts different families, Srey says. "They are related to us as well."

The Leverett temple may be inconvenient for some elders, some of whom don't drive and still struggle to adjust to American culture and forbidding New England winters, Kenseth acknowledges, but it was personally selected by Gosananda. The supreme patriarch of Buddhism in Cambodia and a 1996 Nobel Peace Prize nominee, he lived on the property from time to time and chose this place where the two great Buddhist traditions, northern and southern, could have homes side by side.

Besides, Kenseth says, "When people come onto the land, young and old alike, they say to me, 'Elaine, this reminds me of my country.'"

Srey adds, "At home in Cambodia, it is very common to have a temple in the mountains." Its remoteness adds to its attractiveness for Cambodians, who come for summer retreats from Lowell and elsewhere.

⊠ ⊠ ⊠

Dona Oduc, who moved to the Leverett area in 1992 after training to be a Buddhist nun in the Cambodian temple outside Lowell, remembers arriving and meeting Yae Won, a blind nun who climbed up into a tree to pray.

Oduc, who visits the temple for dharma teachings from the monks and to offer them informal English lessons, says the temple has provided a refuge for people who arrived in a strange land shocked and traumatized by a horrible war.

"They had a beautiful life in Cambodia, but it was completely disrupted," she says. From the time it opened, "People coming through temple doors were really seeking to be counseled out of the insanity they'd been exposed to, back to some state that was calm and peaceful.

"They were not well. Their country had been torn apart; their lives were torn apart. Villages were burned, women were raped, their relatives were murdered. Their most immediate response was total forgiveness. That's their wellness."

At the heart of the temple is Buddha, whose central teaching of forgiveness and compassion is the glow of Watkiry Vongsa.

When she traveled to Cambodia with Gosananda, Kenseth recalls, "I saw how much reverence the people had, and I was always, always moved. I felt the anguish of what they had gone through, yet I saw how sweet they were."

Although she's been less involved in the community in recent years, Kenseth remembers gatherings at which someone would quietly tell her, "You see that man across the room? That's the one who killed my father."

There have been isolated times, too, when Kenseth has witnessed anger well up in a member of the community.

"Others would surround them and say, 'It's alright brother. We'll take care of you.'"

photo by Cara Moser

Barry Moser, engraver

Burdened Brothers

October 9, 2015

I've long been fascinated by the sheer power of Barry Moser's engravings as illustrations for a number of books, including the Bible, the Passover Haggadah, *and the* Wizard of Oz. *I had interviewed him earlier for the Landscape of Creativity series, which appears in* Inner Landscapes. *When this memoir of growing up in a conflicted relationship with his brother in Tennessee showed up in the newsroom, it resulted in this article.*

❋ ❋ ❋

It's a steamy hot Tennessee day for a six-year-old boy, as Barry Moser remembers the time his mother took him shopping in downtown Chattanooga.

In pre-air-conditioned 1946, the doors of the big department store are open, and young Barry, after whining that he's hot and very thirsty, spots two drinking fountains. There's one marked "Whites only" with a long line of thirsty waiting customers, and another, marked "Colored" with no line.

"So I break away from my mother and run for that water fountain. And she goes and gets me, picks me up in her arms, and pulls the boy away from the taboo fountain. I ask her why, and she says, 'Well, honey. Never drink out of that water fountain.'

"That's it. That's the end of my question. When your mama tells you something and you're six years old, you believe her. That's the Word of God."

But Moser, who will mark his seventy-fifth birthday with an opening reception for an R. Michelson Galleries exhibit next week, reveals in his new memoir, *We Were Brothers,* that his mother's friendship with their black neighbor, Verneta Gholston, helped him begin to question an entire way of life.

"Her affection for Verneta was palpable," says the bald, white-bearded author during a recent interview in his Hatfield kitchen about his memoir. "Those two women were really, really good friends, and I suppose that may have laid the groundwork for my divorcing myself from all that and helping me begin my road to recovery" from a childhood surrounded by racism and anti-Semitism.

Moser's 183-page book, just published by Algonquin Press, is a simple yet universally familiar telling of a strained sibling relationship. Tensions run deep not only between the author and his three-year-older, bullying brother Tommy but also with his Tennessee upbringing in a racist, xenophobic family and a culture of bigotry.

The author, who left the South in 1965 to teach art at Williston Academy in Easthampton and went on to become a National Book Award winning author and illustrator, began to reconcile with his brother shortly before Tommy's 2005 death in Nashville.

Among the heart-wrenching stories in *We Were Brothers*— illustrated with Moser's own engravings—is one that tells of Verneta, who used to come across Shallowford Road to the Moser house with Barry's aunts and uncles next door, knocking on the front door to visit if there were no signs of other people around . . . or going to the back if there were.

She was banging frantically on the front screen door as Moser's parents played canasta with family and friends. Earlier in the day, the Ku Klux Klan rampaged up the road, harassing blacks to "Never forgit yore place."

In terror, Verneta forced the door open and burst into the house, sobbing, "What'm I gonna do?" as nearly everyone kept playing and insisted that she simply go away.

Only his mother left to help Verneta back home that day.

"That truly was an epiphany," recalls Moser. "I was a junior in high school. To see that sable skin of hers turn gray, I'll never forget . . . coupled with my Uncle Floyd telling her, 'You're interrupting our card game,' completely insensitive to it. . . . I think about it today and I'll start crying about it."

It wasn't until Moser was in his teens that he started trying to make sense of the injustices he saw around him—prevailing Jim Crow era attitudes that he took for granted and bought into and which his brother seemed to maintain.

He had been about four when Verneta picked him up to take him on a bus to the amusement park with Tommy, and he began to cry and scream.

"Why, honey, what's got into you?" she asked him.

"I said to her, 'I'm afraid that black's going to rub off on me.'" Verneta told him, years later when he went to visit his former neighbor on her porch after his family had moved away.

"I was trying to make sense of it, and it doesn't make sense. It just simply doesn't," recalls Moser. "We had no problem with individual Black people unless they were uppity. The same thing was true with Jews and Catholics."

One vignette in *We Were Brothers* that reflects that attitude toward Blacks is about someone they called Nigger Tommy, the Black boy about Barry's age who showed up one day while the brothers were playing in their yard and was allowed to visit and play with them as long as he didn't come into their house. He was accepted but eventually disappeared, only to reappear working as a carhop at a drive-in restaurant when Moser returned to visit years later with his wife and children.

After Moser had moved to Massachusetts, his brother lit into him when he related how he'd gotten lost near the George Washington Bridge driving down to visit for Christmas.

"There was a long silence, and he said, 'Are you telling me that you live *NORTH* of New York City? When are you gonna move back down here?'

"I said, 'Probably never, Tommy.'

"And he said, 'You better, 'cause all those Jews, Niggers, Dagos, and Wops are gonna take over up there.' Those four."

"All bigotry is ignorant," Moser adds. "His bigotry was particularly ignorant. That's what leaves me believing, in the final analysis, that he was egging me on, mashing my buttons. He knew what would get me upset. And he just kept at it."

In the end, Moser learned that, years later, his brother had become the champion and protector of a Black child adopted by someone in the family, taking him to Little League games and spending time with him.

※ ※ ※

Tommy Moser, who had been held back in first grade because he suffered amblyopia in one eye and then held back again in second grade, seemed to take out his anger over his younger brother "gaining" on him in school. It was a stigma exacerbated by his peers at the military academy both Mosers attended deriding him as "son" or "boy." And then his parents egged him on: "Better watch out, Tommy. Barry's gonna catch up to you."

Tommy repeatedly beat up his younger brother, although they shared a love for their parents, for dogs, and for joking around, Moser recalls.

"I loved my brother and just always wished that he loved me, and I never got that feeling of reciprocation, of affection. I think he did, but I think his ability to express affection, especially toward me, was stunted. I think those three years' difference between our ages and his being only one year ahead of me in school really did a number on him."

Moser's older brother later became successful as a local banker.

But the text of a letter in *We Were Brothers* shows Tommy was in awe of Barry, the celebrated author, illustrator, and designer of more than three hundred books, including Lewis Carroll's *Alice in Wonderland*, for which he won the National Book Award for design and illustration in 1983. Moser, whose other books, published by his Pennyroyal Press, include *Through the Looking Glass, Moby Dick* and *The Bible*, has been on the faculty of Rhode Island School of Design and Smith College. His works have been displayed at the National Gallery of Art, the Metropolitan Museum, the British Museum, the Library of Congress, the National Library of Australia, the Vatican Library, and at Harvard, Yale, Dartmouth, Cambridge, Princeton, and other university museums.

After fifteen years of reflecting on *We Were Brothers*—which Algonquin edited down from nearly five hundred pages and which

Moser plans to issue later in a limited edition published by his own Pennyroyal Press— the author says, "That's the conclusion I've come to: he just couldn't bring himself to put his arms around me. He'd put his arm around me, alright, and slug me in the face."

Moser focuses late in the book on the reconciliation with his brother that took place a few years before Tommy's death. It was prompted by a December 1997 phone call that grew increasingly heated over Moser's use of the word Black when his older brother insisted on saying nigger.

"We still call 'em niggers down here," Tommy said, causing Moser to slam the phone down with instructions never to call back.

A series of letters follows: an angry one from Moser explaining, "It saddens me beyond anything you can imagine that you, my brother, are the purebred and banal embodiment of all the things I hate." He describes the pain of trying to tolerate years of listening to his brother's racial epithets and slurs against women. Four months later, there's a revealing response:

"Barry, I know everything about you, and you know nothing about me," Tommy writes. "I proudly display your works in my home and office, and tears filled my eyes when you were on the *Today* show. I watched all of *Huckleberry Finn* just to see your name in the credits at the end. I have framed the articles that were in *People* magazine and *Newsweek* and *American Artist*. I do love you. Just, Tom P.S. Don't grade this letter."

To that letter, there was an embracing response from Moser followed by phone conversations once or twice a month and a visit with his wife with Tommy and his family in Nashville in 2002 before Tommy's death from cancer stemming from his bad eye less than three years later.

⌗ ⌗ ⌗

In his studio, Moser keeps three photographs that he took at the insistence of his brother.

One shows Tommy standing alone wearing a Baylor School varsity track T-shirt and track shorts. A second shows Tommy on one knee in a classic football portrait pose, wearing a football jersey, pants, and shoulder pads, and holding a football— the kind of shot that lined the gym at Baylor, where "football itself is a religion" as in much of the South. The third photo also shows Tommy on one knee, holding a rifle and a deer head by one of its antlers.

"He never played varsity football," reveals Moser, "the deer was one that hung on the wall in our den, and he's backed up into some brush next to a ditch behind our house. He always wanted to be something that he wasn't. He tried to be a great athlete, and he wasn't a great athlete any more than I was. He so desperately wanted to be something he couldn't be."

One of the photos, though, is truly prescient, Moser adds.

"He lived out the latter part of his life as a very successful big-game hunter," his den filled with "the head and hoof of every hoofed animal that roamed the North American continent, and he was well on his way to collecting all of the African animals."

At his funeral, Moser recounts in his book, the presiding minister delivered a eulogy recalling Tommy's days playing football at Georgia Tech and his nephew reacting later, "That's just like Daddy. He'd tell a story and it'd be about this big . . . and then it'd be *this* big, and before long, he'd get to believing it himself."

▩ ▩ ▩

Moser left the South in 1967 with the Civil Rights era at the time sparking a trail of arguments with family members and others.

But he doesn't believe that the North is necessarily less racist than the South.

"Here in New England, I encounter racism and racist comments from people as much as I do when I'm in the South. It's disguised a little bit better—it's under the surface, but it's there. I go back down to Dixie, and I think of where the South was when I left in 1967 in terms of race relations and where Boston was in 1967, and Dixie has come a long, long way, while Boston hasn't moved very far. I think we delude ourselves in so many ways."

Moser recently discovered a Bible he'd used during a two- or three-year period in college, preaching in the Methodist Church near Chattanooga. The Bible includes notes for a sermon dated 1963.

"I needed to get out of the South because I was saying things from the pulpit that weren't going over very well. I was at odds with my family, at odds with my church, at odds with my society, at odds with the school where I was teaching. I just had to get out."

Moser—who would soon give up the ministry and now considers himself "a deeply religious agnostic"—recalls being an assistant pastor in charge of a youth group and being blamed because a member had gotten pregnant at a church retreat he was supervising.

"The only place that young girl was welcome in the church was in my Sunday school class," he says. She and her boyfriend were ostracized from sitting with the congregation. "I just don't read the Bible that way."

The real epiphany came around the same time, when Moser was invited by John, the Black chef at the country club his stepfather managed, to visit the Baptist church where he served as a deacon.

"My daddy would kill me—and you too," Moser remembers responding, after which it was suggested that he didn't have to tell him. So he drove down to the church, where "'I'm the only white face within a half-mile radius," to be greeted by the minister as Barry Holmes, identified by the chef using the surname of Moser's stepfather.

"No, you don't," the Black pastor told him when he went to sit in the pew beside John. "No man of God's going to sit out there with all those sinners. You're going to sit up here with me!"

No sooner had Moser sat at the dais with the choir behind him and the Black congregation seated in front of him and the women adorned with peach-colored, rose-colored, yellow, and white hats than he was introduced as a special guest who would lead the church in prayer.

"Brothers and sisters, we have the Reverend Barry Holmes with us this morning. He's going to give the morning prayer."

Moser, who was surprised to find he was going to be leading a prayer before an African-American congregation he was attending for the first time, began "Almighty Father . . . "

"Amen," rang back the first of many enthusiastic responses from the church.

"It was wonderful," Moser remembers. "In John's church, I was embraced. Not just welcomed. I was embraced. If John had gone to my church, he would have been lynched in the front yard. I left Chattanooga three or four years later."

❖ ❖ ❖

Moser, whose belt buckle reveals his nickname Bubba, is left to regret that he and Tommy didn't reconcile their differences earlier and to reflect on what might have happened if they'd had more time to enjoy together the things they shared, including their dogs or their humor.

"That's the thing that, had he lived, would have been the cement of our relationship," Moser maintains. "The love of telling funny stories."

21

He's also left to wish that there had been more correspondence between them.

"I wish he had written me more letters. That's the one thing I rue," Moser says. "I'm as much to blame as he. The damn telephone. You pick up the telephone, it's a hell of lot easier than writing a letter. But you don't have the record of it anymore."

The record that's left, mostly, is Moser's compassionate and intimate telling, although he apologizes that some of the details may be clouded by the decades that have passed.

"I'm truly sorry that your Daddy ain't around to read this memoir," he wrote his nephews a couple of years back. "I'm rough on him here and there, but I'm rough on myself, too. . . . But hey, that's what a troubled brotherhood is about."

Wang Hui-Ming, Montague calligrapher

photo by Paul Franz

Brush with Poetry

December 29, 2004

Across the road from the Montague Bookmill, an old sprawling riverside factory building crammed with books, Wang Hui-Ming lived quietly in a home filled with books and Asian artworks, with a small studio in the rear. I can't recall how I learned about the seemingly reclusive master calligrapher but was intrigued by his art and charmed throughout our hourlong conversation.

▩ ▩ ▩

"You must read this," advises eighty-two-year-old master calligrapher and artist Wang Hui-Ming, chuckling and tapping the cover of the book he's holding in his Montague Center home as though each tap secretly sends a silent barb to a particular friend.

Dominated by a large, whimsical oil painting, Wang's living room, like much of the early eighteenth-century house, is peppered with artwork and calligraphy by Wang, who taught at the University of Massachusetts from 1964 to 1988.

"Somebody asked me, 'Why do you paint that painting?' I told him, 'To fill up the place.'"

The "place"—to which Wang moved from Amherst in 1972—has special resonance for the emeritus professor. It dates back to 1956 when he visited a J. P. Morgan Library exhibit of the hundred greatest books of all time. There he found a rare copy of *The Centaur*, a book heralded as a landmark in typography—published in 1915 in Montague.

Published by The Montague Press at the Dyke Mill, it was a translation by George B. Ives of an 1835 prose poem by Maurice de Guérin. Only 135 copies of the 8-page work were printed, according to Yale University Library.

"I saw that book, and I was so moved," says Wang, who felt when he arrived in Amherst that he was close to something of a literary shrine.

"I said, 'I am very close. Why not try to find a place like that? If they published a book like that in China or Japan, that whole town would be called holy.'"

Born in Wuhu, south of Nanjing, Wang served the US Army as a translator during World War II to help train Chinese cadets. He earned an economics degree from the University of Missouri in 1949 as Mao Tse-tung brought China under Communist control.

"You know Chairman Mao—everybody thought of him as a robber and rough guy," says Wang. "He wrote beautiful poems. "When he was seventeen, eighteen, he already had published poetry."

Wang, who translated Mao's poetry in 1975—a work that earned recognition from the American Academy of Poets at the Guggenheim Museum—had taught at Yale University's Institute of Foreign Language for a decade beginning in 1951. He earned a master's degree in economics from New York University in 1953. During those years, he worked as a dishwasher in a Chinese restaurant and lived in Brooklyn, where he met his Cleveland-born wife, Anna.

The playful paintings, imaginative woodcuts, and intricate Oriental and Western calligraphic works that cover Wang's walls and fill some of the hundreds of books shelved and stacked throughout his home make a singular, obvious statement: visual art and written word are one.

"There is painting in poetry; there is poetry in painting," Wang says simply. "They are both related to expressions of the human being. The action itself is beautiful. That's where poetry and painting come from."

In fact, the separation that Western culture insists on imposing between calligraphy and art, between painting and poetry, makes little sense to Wang, whose books of poetry by Robert Bly, James Tate, Robert Francis, and other writers represent far more than illustration.

He points to one framed calligraphic work depicting a fisherman beside a river with fish moving downstream, then getting caught. Here, again, words and pictographs merge.

"The construction of Chinese words is derived from picture first," he explains. "Children can read it because it's a picture. Calligraphy and paintings, you cannot separate it."

The late poet William Stafford put it this way: "In the work of Wang Hui-Ming, does the poem choose design or does design choose the poem? We cannot tell, but together the effect is one of striking harmony. Life comes through to us—important things put into the center again—for us to meet with surprise and delight."

Wang's paintings, meanwhile, are joyous expressions that occasionally incorporate the written word. "To be or not to be," says a 1981 work. "That is the infinitive."

"This is a naughty one," says the self-taught artist, his time-worn face breaking again into a beaming smile as he points to a painting that plays with a nude form.

Hundreds of Wang's paintings and woodcuts fill a giant, unheated studio where he creates prolifically during warmer months. One painting, which seems inspired by calligraphy, measures ten by seven feet.

"If you are born as a writer or painter, you have no way to stop it," he says, displaying his array of artwork.

❖ ❖ ❖

Wang, who has been a fellow of the MacDowell Colony artist retreat in Peterborough, New Hampshire, and has exhibited throughout this country and Canada, has published an array of books, including *The Boat Untied and Other Poems, The Birds and the Animals,* and Robert Bly's *Jumping Out of Bed.*

Called a master by the late artist Leonard Baskin, Wang practices calligraphy each morning at a desk in his bedroom. It's a habit he began at age five under the strict supervision of his father.

"My father had one simple rule: First you get up, wash your face, and write calligraphy before you eat breakfast. If you don't write, you don't eat."

No wonder Wang had little patience for students—in Providence, in Putney, in Amherst, in New Haven—who complained about having to practice, begging to know the practical value of doing so.

"I told my classes, 'You don't come to class to learn art; you go home and paint it.' They ask me, 'How soon will we finish the course?' The modern American youths' concept of time is different from mine in my old age. Nothing good comes easily."

Indeed. Wang's long-term dream has been to teach calligraphy to students in the town where Carl P. Rollins's Montague Press published *The Centaur.* He has approached librarians and others about offering a course free of charge that would end with students producing their own small books. In each case, he's felt rebuffed.

"I moved to this town. My biggest hope was to teach calligraphy and some poetry," Wang says. "I want to revive the honor of Montague because it published *Centaur.* My tears are coming out."

He wipes his eyes and laments.

"Americans are too busy. My father taught me, 'A lifetime is rather short to do something great.' In modern American life, there is no such thing as leisure. If people have nothing to do, they get bored. If they do the classic thing—" and here Wang breaks into the sing-song of his timeless, native tongue. His translation flows, uninterrupted—"your heart is on level, and your breathing is smooth."

In the winter of a vibrant life, looking back to a culture half a world away where elders and calligraphy were venerated, Wang recalls in Chinese the couplet that graced the gates of his childhood home. He sings each phrase as his right hand paints bold brush strokes in the air.

Then he translates.

"Even if I were poor, I would not sell my books, so my children could read them. Even when I am old, I still want to plant bamboo to share the shade with my friends."

❂ ❂ ❂

Wang Hui-Ming died in 2006.

Hawa Tarawally, activist

Taking a Bold Stand for African Girls

April 29, 2017

I first encountered Hawa Tarawally while covering a story about a Congressional candidate's visit to the local community college. While there, I was so impressed with this student's articulate and impassioned questioning of the candidate that I struck up a conversation with her afterward and realized I had to interview her for her own profile. She has since gone on to graduate from Smith College, where she interned in the District of Columbia's Office of Human Rights and as an ambassador to the United Nations Youth Summit.

❀ ❀ ❀

At twenty-two, Hawa Tarawally has seen more of life's struggles than many of her fellow Greenfield Community College students could imagine.

27

Now living in Montague, she left her native Sierra Leone behind last November to escape government retribution for leading a campaign to end the way young girls in her West African country are treated. But she hasn't curtailed her efforts to end forced marriage for young girls and other sexually related abuses in her native land.

"I have been an activist in Sierra Leone since I was ten years old," she says with a self-assurance that makes the defiant, outspoken young woman stand out, just as she stood out last spring at a United Nations youth summit.

Tarawally, who at age two suffered the death of her mother in Sierra Leone's 1997 civil war because the woman had allegedly supplied rebels with food, went on to live with her father in their southeastern village of Kenema Field. Yet, he was unable to care for her.

Her widowed father began drinking, she remembers, "so nobody was really there to take care of me. I was taking care of myself. At four, five years old, I was working in the house, cleaning, but nobody washed me."

Eventually, convinced that he couldn't care for her properly, her father brought her to stay with his younger sister. "But that woman treated me like a dog. When I was staying with her, I had a rash all over my body. I couldn't walk straight because of the rash."

Her father came to take the girl back, bringing her first to a hospital for treatment. She lived with him, her older brother, and other relatives until she was ten.

But "nobody was taking care of us. You take care of yourself."

Around that time, influenced by Network Movement for Justice and Development peer educators in her school, Tarawally became aware of girls around her initiated in female genital mutilation, FGM, and married off by their families at a young age. Boys around them also sexualized the girls, often getting them pregnant or making them susceptible to HIV and AIDS.

"I decided to leave that town before I got pregnant or before I got initiated, or before my family gave my hand into marriage."

Following on the path of the peer educators, Tarawally says, "We promised to them that we would spread what we had learned, and I was raising awareness among my colleagues."

In the aftermath of the civil war, most families that had lost members tried to rebuild by seeing to it that their daughters got pregnant.

"In a society that is full of child abuses," she would tell other girls, "you have to be brave, you have to be assertive, you have to be smart. You have to know how to negotiate with people, to tell them that, 'You know, my daddy really wants me to get married, but please give me some time for me to get some knowledge, to understand what the world is made of.'"

"I was trying to tell them how we can benefit from education instead of allowing our parents to really push us into getting married," says Tarawally, who also tried to spread awareness about the risks of HIV and AIDS.

She attended workshops sponsored for girls by human rights organizations, "talking about these things. I was listening. I would not just go there to eat their food. That's what most of us went there for. I mostly went there to get the knowledge, because by then I was the only girl in my town privileged to be in secondary school. All girls my age were pregnant. So I really, really wanted to make use of the opportunity by focusing and really getting the points and really relating this to my life. And that's what I pretty much did."

Often beginning for girls around age eight, female cutting, as female genital mutilation sometimes is called, is a ritual passage from childhood in her Mandingo ethnic group and others.

It was banned for three years during the country's Ebola crisis and has been the subject of restrictions for girls younger than eighteen. The laws are seldom enforced because of political pressure from guilds of women cutters and cut women throughout much of the country. The ritual practice, named for the prestigious cultural group Bondo, continues as a powerful tradition despite growing calls for an outright ban.

Tarawally says, "They marry girls off from twelve on. I was really tall for my age, ten, so there was potential for me to be given into marriage. The Mandingo and Fula tribes actually plan marriage for you. Your dad doesn't even necessarily need to approve it. When your dad's elder brother says 'yes,' the dad cannot say 'no.'"

It was time to move on, Tarawally decided. So when her father's younger brother came to visit from Kenema, a city of about two hundred thousand, she told him, "Uncle, I'm going with you. You're not going to leave me here."

She grabbed her bag, climbed onto his motorcycle, and moved to the city, where she says his wife verbally abused her and fed her burned rice before finally asking her to return to her village "where I knew I would be given into marriage and would be subjected into FGM. Maybe I would get pregnant. I would never go back to that village!"

"My uncle said, 'Well, you have to leave my house,'" so at age eleven or twelve, she began living with friends, going from house to house to stay during the next year or two.

Along the way, the young teen met Ann-Marie Caulker of the National Movement for Emancipation and Progress, a coalition campaigning against harmful practices. Caulker was a co-founder of Katanya Women's Development Association, KaWDA, along with Marina Goldman of Montague. Goldman has worked on women's health issues in Sierra Leone during about a dozen trips since 2007.

KaWDA, created in 1996, works to empower women and children in Sierra Leone by providing access to education, skills training, and support "to build a strong and resilient society," according to its website.

Caulker "became like a mom to me."

The girl began living with her cousin and being cared for by Caulker until age fifteen, when she took her high school entrance exam.

"My uncle told my dad that somebody intoxicated my brain, that a woman mixed up my brains and wanted me to get pregnant and be a prostitute and that woman was not really a good person." So her father, along with family members including her aunts and grandmother, went to Caulker and brought Tarawally to the tribal leader.

The leader ordered her returned to the custody of her family.

But her grandmother, with whom she was forced to live in Kenema, "misled me," sending her to get something from a friend who lived in the bush, remembers Tarawally.

"I went there, and that's when they initiated me in the ritual mutilation," tying her down and blindfolding her. "I was very frightened—and very angry."

The next morning, the girl was awakened and told that the painful cutting would have to be done again because it had been too dark at night to do correctly.

After that, "They laid their hands on me. They really wanted to do things as fast as they could. They wanted to give my hand in marriage," despite her father's opposition. Rather than consenting to a forced marriage, the sixteen-year-old girl hid and escaped, relocating to Bo, Sierra Leone's second-largest city. There, Caulker helped support her and sent her to high school.

Tarawally did so well in school and on her university entrance exam that she was admitted to the University of Sierra Leone's Fourah Bay College—"a university that is very hard to get admitted into, especially if you're coming from the provinces."

Focused on political science, Tarawally was invited in her second year to a United Nations youth summit along with students from Gambia, Kenya, Europe, and Asia. From March to August, she traveled around the United States and learned from other students that a key would be registering the organization she'd already created back home, Every Step Counts, to help girls like herself.

"At the end of the day, I got a lot of inspiration to go back and see how I could legally register my own foundation and really go back to my activities on a different level that time around." Tarawally had been "scared of victimization, scared of oppression. But when I came to the US and saw incredibly outstanding youths and talked with them and actually learned what they had been doing in their different countries and how they had been successful, I decided to go back home" and work to raise awareness about female genital mutilation.

"That's the thing nobody really wants to talk about," she says of an aspect of tradition that politicians use to win votes. "You can stand up for what you believe in, but . . . " she pauses, "they will oppress you, either by torturing you, defaming you unlawfully, taking you to the prisons or beating you up, or just kidnapping you … and all of a sudden, you disappear."

She adds, "It's forbidden for somebody who's been through FGM, like myself, to stand up and oppose it. You don't do it. If you do, the law is you will be re-initiated. You will be re-cut!"

Nonetheless, with her foundation registered, Tarawally returned to activism, going into schools, to rundown neighborhoods housing the poor and talking to parents and students there.

And then to really draw attention to her message, she organized a flash mob on November 12, her twenty-second birthday, playing music and dancing out on the streets with other people joining in.

"We are actually dancing in the streets. All of sudden, I would just take my shirt off like this, and you see the other shirt underneath say, 'Stop FGM and Child Marriage.'"

Three days later, she was awakened by a knock at her door, and three men asked for her with a warrant to take her to the police station. They offered no reason, telling her only that it came "from above."

"I was so worried, because I have my dad, my brother, my stepmom, my siblings. I was so worried about them." Tarawally was detained for four days and eventually allowed to send for her brother after telling the authorities she needed her food and medicine.

One of the authorities told her brother that her detention had been "a warning shot," and her brother advised Tarawally to "refrain from whatever it is that I'm doing."

She asked, "'Warning shots for what? What did I do?' I wasn't thinking about what I had done the previous days, the flash mob. I didn't know they had access or any connection to that. I wasn't thinking about that!"

Then, on November 24, she learned that another activist from her university had been arrested for sharing a social media post about an upcoming demonstration.

In response, "I went to different colleges in (the capital city) Freetown and said, 'We all need to go out in our numbers tomorrow and protest against what has happened. Otherwise, this is going to keep on happening, and a lot of young people are going to keep on being detained or being arrested for no reason. Nobody will have the right to say whatever it is they know is wrong!'"

The protest in front of the courthouse drew about a hundred individuals, according to an article in the *Guardian*.

"In the past two years, the country's ruling party has shown a worsening, often violent intolerance for public criticism, and with an eleven-year civil war in the rearview mirror, a culture of silence often deters would-be protesters from publicly airing their grievances," the newspaper said. "But in the past week, (student Theresa) Mbomaya's case has quickly evolved into a cause célèbre that, bolstered by the country's grim economic conditions, has become the epicentre of a growing social movement calling for unobstructed freedom of expression. . . . Since the height of the Ebola outbreak, opposition members, protesters, activists, and journalists have been jailed, beaten, tear-gassed, or shot for publishing material or staging demonstrations deemed critical of government policy."

Following the protest, Tarawally received a text message from one of the men who had detained her, warning: "If you know what is good for you, find somewhere to go for now. You can go to Liberia. Just go straight there for now. This place is not safe for you, for now."

Tarawally had visited the United States a few months earlier and had no thoughts of returning so soon, even though Caulker had invited her to attend a December 2 global summit in Washington, DC, to end violence against women and girls.

"But when this happened, I said, 'I think I have to go. I have to go to this event and'"—banging her knuckles on the table in front of her with each syllable for emphasis—"'I might not come back.'"

So, she returned to the US, where she began taking classes at Greenfield Community College.

Tarawally has since launched a change.org petition to the UN to ban female genital mutilation and forced marriages.

At the conference, "I told everybody how they treat young people—youths and activists—in Sierra Leone and in Africa as a whole. How they suppress us. How we the youths don't have any freedom of speech. Activists don't have rights to say the truth. They will be oppressed and suppressed by political leaders. FGM is a global issue. So please make global laws, laws that will be able to defend and protect activists from all over the world. I told them everything because I knew I wasn't going back.

"I knew here I will be able to get justice," Tarawally says. "Keeping silent would just kill me."

Singers gather daily on Montague Town Common

Singing on Common Ground

April 30, 2021

Here's an instance where my own passion for music developed into a story. A year after I'd retired and COVID-19 sent communities into lockdown, I began joining the daily outdoor singing sessions that sprang up spontaneously on my own town common. There were just a handful of us that snowy March, and the uniqueness of what we found ourselves enjoying just as spontaneously spawned this article.

❊ ❊ ❊

It sounds crazy, but Montague has been singing every single day since COVID-19 lockdowns began two years ago.

Not the entire town, of course. But still, it seems to boggle many minds: the notion of a group with typically eight or more singers on the town common in blizzards, downpours, scorching heat, or sub-zero windstorms each afternoon since March 18, 2020.

"You tell people what we're doing, and they ask, 'When is it? Every Tuesday?'" says Will Quale, a core group member, who set up a TownCommonSongs.org website to help singers keep track of their ever-growing repertoire. "And you correct them and repeat that it's *every day*. It doesn't sink in. It doesn't fit anyone's idea of what's possible."

If the notion of an hour-long daily sing outdoors in this little village is hard to grasp, so is the fact that there is no organization, no leader, and that the ritual began almost by accident.

"Everything had ended," recalls Laurie Davidson, another core group member, remembering her early-morning run on March 15, 2020, when she met up with neighbor Tamara Kaplan. Together, inspired by shut-in Italians making music from balconies, they hatched an idea.

Both women had sung together in Greenfield Harmony, a chorus recently silenced by COVID.

"Wouldn't it be fun to get together and sing? We said, 'Let's do it!'"

Incredibly, a dozen neighbors turned out simply by word of mouth and email for that first 3 p.m. sing on Taylor Hill.

"People were desperate for something," recalls Davidson, for whom singing goes back to when she and her three sisters would perform at nursing homes and around their western Connecticut home.

"Let's do it again," the singers said when it was over. And so they returned, this time to the Montague Town Common. Standing in a large circle ten feet apart and mostly unmasked, a group of a dozen or so neighbors showed up to sing whatever struck their fancy. The spontaneity continued one afternoon following the next, all by consensus every step of the way.

"We've found some sort of delightfully unorganized consistency somehow," observes Quale, who has an ethnomusicology degree and has led pub singing for years in Brattleboro, Vermont, and elsewhere. "We have this very egalitarian, open format where no one's giving it direction, and a whole lot of people are giving it enthusiasm."

In fact, that may be a secret to the success of what just may be the only ongoing, daily outdoor community sing of its kind anywhere. And mind you, this is New England, where winters can be blustery and downright cold.

"Everyone seems to be really good at listening to everyone else, figuring out what's good for the group. And that's magic. I don't know how we do it," says Quale, for whom the daily sings have been "a lifeline—a steadying, constant presence that's gotten me outdoors, often in the sunshine for about an hour, socializing with a nice community of friends. When I went into hibernation, the singing got me out."

Unlike monthly pub singing, the daily gatherings have allowed the group to build a repertoire of sometimes more complex songs, which Quale likes.

"Here, I'm constantly having the opportunity to push myself to try that song, to go out on that limb and try it, and 'Now, let's sing another one.' And I love that."

More than 360 songs are currently on the TownCommonSongs. org site, with lyrics, historical background, and links to video performances. Quale guesses that as many other songs already sung have yet to be listed.

The songs, requested randomly by singers as the mood suggests, includes plenty of titles everyone knows, like "This Land is Your Land" or '"Here Comes the Sun." But there are also folk songs, freedom songs, rounds, inspirational anthems, or Broadway favorites.

Few of the songs are sung to printed song sheets or arranged music.

There are camp songs, hymns, and anthems like Si Kahn's "Here is My Home," seasonal songs like "Mud, Mud," and nature songs about skunks or worms, wind, or water.

"There's no filter for what's acceptable," says Tim Van Egmond, a storyteller and contradance musician who's sung folk songs professionally for years. "It really does run the gamut. There are so many songs I'm so glad I learned there that I didn't know about.

"Once I started coming, I thought, 'Oh my god! What a treasure!' There's 'Let Union Be in All Our Hearts,' which is almost a theme song because it's so in line with what the general sentiment is. There are the inspiring songs and the ones that are very spiritual or the really fun ones that have motions that go with them. It's what everybody brings to it. It's so community based."

If that seems like a wondrous therapy to the daily ritual, that may be because of its organic and egoless nature.

"It's the way everybody listens to each other, appreciates each other," Van Egmond says. "You don't have leaders and followers. Everybody is making space for each other. There's nobody interested in being a star or getting a spotlight more than anybody else. Everybody has the space to think of a song," sometimes looking around to see who can lead it or remember words. Sometimes it's a matter of Googling the title on cellphones or checking the website or a copy of the *Rise Up Singing* songbook.

Although many of the singers who've come from Montague and beyond have sung before in various choruses, Van Egmond says, "Here it's just people who basically said, 'We want to sing.'"

And yet it's also more.

"We sing songs," Quale says, "but we also sing our pain, our joy, our worry, our solidarity, our uncertainty, our hope through choosing particular songs or for the way we lead them. When I lead a song and other voices join in, I feel heard, and I don't feel like I have to face that pain or hold that hope alone. It's collaborative therapeutic art, and we've all gotten really good at listening to each other."

From minute to minute over the course of an hour of singing beneath the church's clock tower—inspiring periodic singing of "ring out, bells of Montague"—it's hard to know what song, or even what type of song, will be next to pop up on the day's hit parade. It's also impossible to predict who'll show up, young or old.

"It's extremely unpredictable what we'll be singing," says fifteen-year-old Solena Davidson Carroll, who often joins her mother at the sings and is a veteran of several area choruses. "It's kind of mysterious, kind of captivating. It could really be anything."

Though at the outset there were just a few shared songs, there's now a solid core with additions suggested daily.

"You feel you know all these songs, but you go, and somebody has a new song, and you completely love it, and it becomes your new favorite," says Davidson Carroll, who offered Taylor Swift's "22" to celebrate February 22, 2-22-22. "For me, having lots of different ages singing is kind of fun, because people have different songs to bring from different places and different times, so they might have a different song they might know that I wouldn't know."

One mashup of songs from the World War I era has participants singing "It's a Long Way to Tipperary," "Keep the Home Fires Burning," and "There's a Long, Long Trail a-Winding."

For Addie Rose Holland, the gatherings offer a chance to sing with her five-year-old daughter, Olive, as well as her father, Ray Holland.

"For Olive, it's this weirdly normalized thing," she says. "I don't think she considers whether this happens in every community or not. She's very keen on every song that's sung and will remember and sing them at home. She may not be singing along, but she's listening closely and internalizing them. She's singing all the time at home. More often than not, it's a song from the sing."

Holland, who recalls singing with her family while growing up in Vermont, says, "I feel incredibly lucky that my dad and my daughter can share this experience. I would go every day if I could," but because of her work schedule, that's limited to weekends and snow days.

"Even though showing up every day for two years is not a simple matter by any stretch, it simplifies it for us to participate and makes it possible, especially since all we have to do is walk down the street. Olive doesn't appreciate the specialness of it as much as I do."

She also brings her daughter to the monthly full-moon singing sessions that have grown out of the daily sings as well as to holiday caroling. Olive, in fact, was the inspiration for a lantern-festooned winter solstice sing in December.

Even in the pouring rain under the church overhang, even on the most wind-chilling New England winter days, the gatherings never get old because every day seems to celebration of something somewhere: Day 300, Day 500, Pi Day on March 14 (3.14), One Million Minutes of songs, "Plough Not Monday," the Perseid meteor shower, even the birthday of a participant's singing father.

The ritual has also spawned special pop-up events, including evening firepit sings, the return of a singer who's gone traveling, Mummers' plays, and special song offerings for Earth Day, Election and Inauguration days, and a Black Lives Matter sing. The Russian invasion of Ukraine was marked by singing Ukraine's national anthem.

"One of things that really works for us, instead of being an old established group from pre-pandemic times that was trying to find a way to sustain ourselves," says Quale, "is that we're just folks in the town coming from a variety of different musical backgrounds, sharing a whole bunch of things that are very new to various other people in the group. For us, having this weird, wonderful smorgasbord of songs from such a variety of places, genres, times—that's just what we do. That's our sound."

⊠ ⊠ ⊠

Although singers come mostly from Montague, guests pop in from time to time, including experienced song leaders like Michael Kline of Sunderland, Ben Fink from Philadelphia, Saro Lynch from Asheville, or Minneapolis songwriter Sarina Partridge, who visited the gathering's seven-hundredth day celebration recently.

"These folks are so amazing, learning and singing these songs with great gusto," she blogged afterwards. "What if every town/city had a standing daily sing. Can you even imagine?!?"

One guest last fall, University of Massachusetts doctoral student Jessica Wiseman, was doing research for her dissertation on community music.

"When I began this study, I thought I would find people preserving folk music. Instead, I found folk music preserving people," Wiseman wrote. Instead of "refined concerts and professional theaters," she discovered "imperfect music by imperfect musicians that provided the perfect outlet for the people of this community."

She questions whether the daily singing would have survived if not for the pandemic, yet "It's about so much more than the music. It's about the community that's created, the hope the group brings, the normalcy the group brings—about a sense of belonging, a sense of security in what are still unprecedented times."

Some believe the quality of the group's ensemble singing has improved through daily practice, but they know that the strength of bonds—even among people who hardly knew one another at the beginning—have deepened.

"We've now shared so many experiences on the common, so there's a lot of shared culture," says Davidson, with singers sometimes knowing by a single word or glance what the next song suggestion will be.

When storms threaten, regulars check to make sure at least someone will show up. Singers have even come together to share Thanksgiving or Christmas meals.

Quale organized the group's website partially as a resource for other communities to follow Montague's example, yet that hasn't happened. It's not clear why the little village has succeeded in creating such a dedicated singing ritual when other communities haven't.

That may have to do with attitude.

"We do have an unusual, I suspect, number of people who've had song leading or music teaching experience or performing experience," Quale says. "Not every village has that."

Not every village has the same rich musical history as a community with people drawn by contradances and fiddle master David Kaynor—who died last June. That's made for the village becoming something of a traditional musical mecca.

People in most places nowadays rarely bring music or dance to daily life, says Quale, and "a lot of people have the sense singing isn't anything they can do except when they're in the shower, in the car, or at church. And when they encounter something like us singing, some approach cautiously, curiously," often apologizing self-consciously that they can't sing and just want to listen. But after a song's chorus repeats, "they begin singing unconsciously. And sometimes, they'll say, 'This is fun. That's a song I remember.' It awakens something. And we'll find it's a closet Gilbert and Sullivan fan or Beatles fan."

Observing the seasons pass and then returning day by day, singers break into a tractor song or one to celebrate truckers or snow plows driving by. They've gathered for birthdays, to mark a hundred and three hundred continuous singing days and for even a small potluck picnic-table Thanksgiving.

They've bonded with the school bus whose arrival signals that the hour-long 2 p.m. sing is drawing to a close.

Singers have even turned out to celebrate the annual nighttime blooming of Davidson's cereus cactus at her home.

For those who pass by waving from their bicycles or honking from their cars, some might wonder how they can get a singing ritual started in their own community.

"Just start," says Davidson. "If you think we need to get this organized or we need ten people to connect or we need a director and his repertoire isn't ready yet, it may never happen.

"All we had to do was just physically show up, and then the songs came out."

photo by Paul Franz

Denise DiPaolo, restaurateur, and Hilton Dottin, chef,
test recipes

Feeding a Dream

May 27, 2006

*Of the twenty-five or so series I wrote during my career
on subjects ranging from nuclear power to sexual abuse to
immigrants from the various former Soviet republics to aging
baby boomers facing a variety of tough choices, this was
perhaps my favorite. I'd met Denise DiPaolo as a community
development specialist, and as soon as I learned she was
working on starting a restaurant, I sensed that writing about
every step of her journey toward her envisioned startup would
make a fascinating story. Based on months of interviews as
her own three-year project took shape, the series ran for six
days and won a First Place Award in the New England Press
Association newspaper contest. This is a first-day sidebar story
in the series. It's followed by the series conclusion.*

41

In Turners Falls, a village of countless bricks, Denise DiPaolo has been cooking up plans to build a new future. The middle-aged single mother of two has been immersing herself in the community where, just this year, she bought a two-story brick Victorian house that overlooks the Connecticut River.

DiPaolo, a former community organizer for Franklin County Community Development Corporation, anticipates a reawakening in the one-time busy mill town.

She's intentionally set down roots here, charting her future and laying down its foundation brick by brick.

Even before being laid off from the community organizing job in 2002, she had begun working with Turners Falls landlords and trying to get downtown residents involved in supporting the businesses there to get the community going again.

Already a member of the Shea Theater board of directors, she also has become active in a Montague Economic Development Task Force. The group is focused on breathing new life into the vacant Strathmore paper mill as restoration of the Colle Opera House and opening of Great Falls Discovery Center suggests a turning point for a Turners Falls economic renaissance.

That's why she moved to town and has been working on a business plan for a restaurant.

Armed with copies of Malcolm Gladwell's book, *The Tipping Point: How Little Things Can Make a Big Difference,* she went before the Montague selectboard and told them the time was right for Turners. And for her.

She proposed turning a rundown, three-story building the town owned on Second Street into her own Back Alley Café Pub. DiPaolo has been talking with potential investors and working with architects about the building, which Montague officials had seized from a previous owner for nonpayment of taxes. They must choose between her and the Northeast Foundation for Children, both competing to buy the building for a dollar in exchange for promises of redevelopment.

DiPaolo has imagined running a café since she was in high school in Pennsylvania. "For thirty years, it's been a dream," she says. When she first saw the vacant Second Street building, she said, "Oh my God! It's an ideal location sitting right by the Shea Theater!"

For two years, she's been writing business plans and talking with friends about the idea and trying to get her life in order. Like many other county entrepreneurs past and present, DiPaolo has always wanted to go into business for herself. But she started having children and found her life had changed.

Her recent layoff from the CDC brought another change, which she's turning to her advantage: she's taken a job as a hostess at the Riverview Cafe in Brattleboro and has begun doing catering in Northampton to learn the restaurant ropes.

Meanwhile, she estimates the Second Street building will cost $150,000 to renovate and $100,000 for startup capital. And she hopes to raise $50,000 in seed money from investors and by selling slate tile, engraved with contributors' names to attach to the building exterior.

The plan is for the basement to become the pub serving micro-brewed beers and for a first-floor café serving "simple, but good food." The second floor would eventually become a space for live music.

She hopes to open her café-pub by fall.

September, 2004

DiPaolo has lost her bid. Northeast Foundation for Children will move its offices from East Greenfield to Second Street.

After spending nearly ten thousand dollars out-of-pocket for a floor plan, contractors' estimates and marketing, DiPaolo has shifted her focus to a long vacant laundromat and soft ice cream place on Avenue A that the town wants to fill with a viable business.

Her proposal for the 166 Avenue A building is the only one the town has received. DiPaolo believes the space and location—"a really sweet spot"—are actually better for what she has re-envisioned as an Italian restaurant.

It's more compact and right on the main street.

"When I ran the numbers, an espresso-based coffee business with pastries really is a volume-based business. You have to get the street traffic of literally thousands of people over the course of a week. That isn't something I think Turners could support at this time."

Harkening back to memories of visiting the farmers market every weekend while growing up in Lancaster, Pennsylvania, and to her own family history, DiPaolo is focused on "simple, fresh, uncomplicated food."

Memories of DiPaolo's great-grandmother, Concietta, keep her well fed. And the matriarch's spunkiness has also been handed down through generations.

"She ruled the roost. She spoke the language," says DiPaolo, recalling frequent visits to a country house where the huge garden yielded a bumper crop of vegetables and where balls of provolone and sticks of salami hung from the ceiling of one of Concietta's two kitchens.

"It was very old world. She never used bowls. She'd just have a heaping pile of flour, make a well in it, crack in a dozen eggs, and whip it with her hand. She'd make gnocchi. She'd have pasta drying over the backs of chairs."

February, 2005

A delicious array of books like *For Cooks Who Love Wine, Chocolate and Coffee,* and *Culinaria Italy* dot DiPaolo's living room. She's on the couch, a cup of coffee in hand, awaiting news about refinancing the house she bought two years ago. A bubbling real estate market has nearly doubled the house value, and interest rates are at a historic low.

This allows DiPaolo to refinance her house to borrow ten thousand dollars toward renovation of the thirty-six-hundred-square-foot Avenue A building, constructed a century ago as a shoe store. The town is willing to sell for a dollar, but it's in bad shape.

"It needs everything. It will be a total gut job with all new everything in it."

That translates into well over $250,000: $170,000 to $180,000 just to renovate the structure and another $100,000 for startup equipment and supplies.

She's approached a couple of potential business investors, each of whom may be willing to put in ten thousand dollars, and she's depending on the CDC to provide gap financing to get the business going.

But bankers, she's learned, aren't head over heels when it comes to very shaky ventures like a restaurant.

"In theory, it's great," she says, "but in actuality, they're not that confident that this is going to go. Most restaurants fail within the first year or two. What makes them not fail? That's the question."

To step up her learning curve on restaurants, she's ended her Brattleboro diner job after less than a year and is now managing

Sunderland's Blue Heron restaurant, a high-end place closer to her vision.

DiPaolo has watched the slowly budding Turners Falls downtown over the past decade and, now that Hallmark Institute has leased the Colle Opera House for a photography museum, she wants to be in business when it blossoms.

"There are no places to eat in Turners. In some ways, it is a big risk. Hopefully, it will influence other businesses to come in and join the ranks." Yet, she adds, "I'm not stupid enough to think, 'Just build it and they'll come.' I have to be creative."

She's been doing her homework. Yesterday, she met with Patrick McCarthy, who owns Jake's restaurant in Northampton and who used to own White Salmon Grill in Sunderland.

"I called him out of the blue because someone said, 'You should talk to this guy,'" says DiPaolo. She showed him her plans, and he offered to examine the financial estimates she's come up with.

"I'm going to have to have more realistic numbers. He's semi-retired and is looking for a new project. I'm in the market for a chef."

The bank and CDC keep advising her to find a chef as a partner, someone willing to invest in the business. "They really want to see somebody else take some risk. If it's somebody I know, who has some reputation, I'd be willing to do that."

Meanwhile, she's thinking about placing an ad on the website of Culinary Institute of America and is starting to put feelers out to see who's available.

DiPaolo's verve and nerve have helped her get this far.

"Every step of the way, I've been sent out with homework assignments: we need to see this, this and this, and you need to get your credit straightened out. I'm sure I've been a pain in the neck to a lot of people just in my perseverance. I've been in people's faces for quite a while now. It's starting to work: they're listening to me," she says.

Greenfield Co-operative Bank Vice President Michael Davey, who knows DiPaolo from when he was on the CDC board, asked her, "Have you considered Amherst for your business?"

She has but figures she couldn't even afford the rent, let alone ever own real estate there.

As a new entrepreneur, DiPaolo keeps bumping up against conflicting sets of full-blown ideas of what her restaurant could be and the realities of the market in this reawakening factory village.

That means studying "what's in vogue, what they're going after, where they're spending their money, what kind of environment they'd like to be in when eating," says DiPaolo of her potential clientele.

"All those kinds of details are really vital, and you have to cater to that."

Her legs folded under her on the couch, she says she wants to make customers feel comfortable when they dine. Yet her plan is for white linen tablecloths. "It will be classy but casual, with impeccable service, with funky, great, warm ambiance."

That funkiness is already tangible, with a pair of mahogany church pews from Charlemont that she bought a couple of years ago at a Deerfield antique shop, now patiently waiting in her foyer.

"I've been collecting furnishings for years," says DiPaolo, who foresees placing them in a courtyard under a canvas awning with tables she'll have built. "It will be a fun place to hang, won't it?"

Her main job will be "to meet and greet and to make people feel they belong and want to be there, that they are welcomed. I want it to feel like my home, like my kitchen, and to have it be a really fun place."

She also knows this won't be the upscale Blue Heron, where she's gotten a rare taste of the prizes and pitfalls of running a top-flight restaurant. Her Turners Falls startup will have to be competitive. Thankfully, overhead in an Italian restaurant can be relatively low.

"Who doesn't love pasta?" she asks. "Hearty, filling food. My menu will be very, very small in the beginning, with a couple or three salads, a couple or three entrees, and some soups. My long-range goal is to get dinnertime successful and add lunch."

Her latest "jumping off point" sample menu has a variety of pastas adding salmon, mussels, clams, or skewered shrimp over pasta. She's also excited by the multicultural possibilities in the village around her: Polish, Irish, Russian specials for lunch, maybe a kielbasa sandwich on the bar menu.

Her Yugoslavian hairdresser Maria offers her grandmother's goulash recipe, and DiPaolo imagines a cook-off contest with winners sampled on the menu or a flavor-filled street fair.

Maybe she can sell beers from around the world as well as a complement of local brews. Maybe a liquor license down the road so she can offer "specialty drinks" like Limoncello to complement the menu with after-dinner liqueurs.

"You know?" she asks. "Stuff like that would be so much fun to do."

photo by Paul Franz

Denise DiPaolo visits with Ristorante DiPaolo customers.

Serving It All Up

May 24, 2006

*Capping my six-day restaurant creation series was this
final story on what became a destination restaurant offering
"traditional authentic Mediterranean-Italian (recipes) with a little
Caribbean flair."*

❋ ❋ ❋

A plate of bow-tie pasta with meatballs and fennel sausage sits in
front of Patricia Pruitt, Montague selectboard member, while behind
her is a twenty-four-foot fresco of raw, layered golds, oranges, reds,
yellows, inspired by a wall along a backstreet in Rome.

A Latin-accented trumpet wails in the background as Denise
DiPaolo, in red satin jacket with black slacks and top, greets invited
guests to a reception celebrating a nearly five-year journey.

As servers dressed in black pass trays of bruschetta and cooked
shrimp with ginger-mango coulis, chef Gilberto "Hilton" Dottin—in
white chef's jacket and black cap—carefully tosses more pasta and
sausage with pomidoro-basil sauce.

With that same sort of attention to detail, DiPaolo and Dottin
have combined colors, sounds, textures and flavors to create Ristorante
DiPaolo. The thirty-five or so people eating and mingling in the candle-
lit space on Avenue A in Turners Falls can hardly imagine the years of

planning, head banging, and scavenging that went into it all nor how completely hopeless the same space seemed just four months earlier.

November 10, 2005

It's been a little over a month since DiPaolo quit her Blue Heron Restaurant manager's job in Sunderland to focus on getting her own bistro up and running.

Jim Fernandes and his construction crew have begun gutting the long-vacant Avenue A building, which the town sold to her for a dollar. They filled a dumpster on just their first day, and now they're onto their third. They're installing a rubber roof, cutting out part of the rear brick wall to put in a delivery entrance, and opening up what will be the main entrance on the side of the building.

The crew is excavating the dirt cellar floor to put in concrete. They've been building up the main floor about five inches to grade and are framing it. Next week, the brick will be cleaned and new glass installed.

The fifty-year-old entrepreneur, too, has been busy. She's designing four chandeliers for a blacksmith friend to make, has ordered two round tables, bought chairs and is finishing work on the menu, adding a pork dish, so it can go to press.

"Things are going great guns. He wants to have me open the week of December 19," she says of Fernandes. "The word's out on the street, and we're getting a lot of curiosity seekers. We can only hold fifty people, and I think we'll be packing the house."

Still, she's looking ahead to a quiet opening, with a grand opening later. Years after starting plans for her dream business, she announces, "We're going to ease into this."

November 21, 2005

The gaudy blue Laundromat/Cree Mee awnings have been removed from the front, the Powertown Cree Mee sign on the front door window is covered with duct tape, and the granite facade below is more prominent.

On the building's side, Fernandes has installed a new sidewalk— with someone mischievously adding DP in the fresh cement—and is preparing a handicapped ramp for what will become the new entrance. A piece of plywood covers the entrance now, but DiPaolo has bought an extra-wide mahogany door with glass panes.

"Very simple, very understated," she says. "I'm spending money up, and the kitchen is being used up."

For contractor Fernandes's four-member crew, it has been three weeks of surprises.

They ran into bricks on the rear wall that needed reinforcement. In the cellar, they found rocky ledge where there should have been soft dirt.

"It's hard work moving things around, but it surprises me how perfect this job has worked out," Fernandes says. "Everyone had questions about whether the labor would be worth it. After one month, it's going to be remarkable."

The biggest surprise has been the weather. But with two days of rain predicted tomorrow and Wednesday, snowfall is due on Thanksgiving.

"It's a dream come true," Fernandes says. He expects his brother to return tomorrow to finish framing the inside in preparation for the heating contractor next week.

Inside, with work lights all around and a construction radio blasting, two masked crew members are on ladders and clawing nails from beams.

The interior walls are all framed. DiPaolo has done away with plans for a coatroom but has opted for two large bathrooms, which she now sees will mean sacrificing space in the kitchen in back.

"It shrunk," she says. "Everything got moved back. One of the refrigerator units may not be able to get in here." It will go down in the cellar, where a large Avenue Laundromat sign still sits on the dirt floor, and where there are plans for a walk-in cooler, dry storage and an office. She also learned that a used dishwasher she bought is probably ten years old, not two as she thought, and may not be able to pump the water she needs.

"I'm running around faster than I was, because I'm having to make quick decisions. I can't sit on them and ponder what to do with the floor, with acoustic tiles. It's happening so fast. I wake up a lot at night."

She may not be able to afford having the carved sign she wants this year and may go with a more subtle painting of her logo on the front windows.

"I'm already cutting corners. The money's just pouring out the door," she says. "Jim's been telling me all along he'll have me up and running before Christmas. Part of me is telling him, 'Great' but not believing it. Part of me is freaking out that he might actually be right."

December 6, 2005

The framing's done inside the Avenue A space, which is beginning to look more like a potential restaurant than a derelict coin laundry. The walls won't be up for another week or so, yet it's clear where the bathrooms are, the bar, the kitchen. The cellar's done, the back brick wall is entirely restored with a service entrance added, and ductwork is started for the heating system.

Three vendors were lined up earlier today to talk with DiPaolo, who's been filling out enough credit applications that she could probably do them in her sleep.

"I've been making a ton of phone calls and meeting salesmen; they've been coming out of the woodwork," says DiPaolo, who's interrupted with calls that strangers are wandering around the work site asking for her.

December 21, 2005

The bar is in place near the entrance with a sunken space for the bartender and a design incorporating seats and the bar itself at the heights of tables and chairs, so someone sitting having a drink would be at the same height as someone standing and having a conversation.

Fernandes first saw the design at the cocktail lounge at Bradley International Airport and talked DiPaolo into incorporating it.

December 27, 2005

Two white Rocky's Acoustics and Acoustical Ceilings trucks are parked in front of 166 Avenue A, where a pair of front windows are boarded up. Just inside, two workers on scaffolding finish work on the aluminum ceiling frame beneath a layer of pink insulation. A pulsating red laser from a self-leveling emitter in one corner lit by hanging work lights sends a virtual plumb line around the room two inches below the ceiling as a portable radio on the floor also pulsates, with rock.

Sunlight pours into the space from the transom. The new furnace pumps out heat. The space is coming into its own.

Four more workers prepare recently installed drywall with primer as Fernandes sits on one of four bare plywood banquettes pointing at a wall: "The bricks will be cleaned up, but not too cleaned up. It's a hundred years old; it needs to look a hundred years old."

DiPaolo walks in, gives Fernandes a kiss and a hug, and exclaims, "Look: a ceiling! It's fantastic! I can't wait to get my plants in here."

Beyond the front room where the plywood floor is raised and the ceiling drops from twelve feet to a more intimate ten feet, the two-by-two-foot tiles are already installed—soon to be painted an earth green to "warm it right up," DiPaolo says. She's pleased that she rejected cheaper, more institutional two-by-four tiles. It's details like those and the outdoor Baltimore lampposts she picked up from a Belchertown antique dealer that are adding ambience to the space —and to its cost.

Fernandes's father, who worked in the steel fabrication business, created base plates outdoors for the five-hundred-pound lampposts, which have been sandblasted and painted black to support the main awning. His brother, a painting contractor, will be in to paint the walls next week, and his two other brothers will be working on the building as well.

DiPaolo has been shopping for light fixtures, fans, furniture, menu covers, fabric for cushions, carpeting, and a black, gold-specked bar top.

"You can do anything with money," she says. The ventilation hood for the kitchen alone was twenty-one thousand dollars. "Can you believe that?" she asks, reflecting on the money she's going through with weeks to go before any income starts coming in. The restaurant was the family's only Christmas present this year.

"I'm really anxious. I still have some kitchen equipment to buy. It's pretty freaky." She looks around the space. "Obviously, there's no turning back now."

With Fernandes talking of a completion date of January 20, DiPaolo has been speaking with prospective employees.

"My son and all his friends want to work. Nick will wash dishes and prep in the kitchen, but he's very adamant about not being a busboy or a runner. Luke is going to start a bartending course.

She and Dottin have also been fine-tuning the menu. They've removed the carpaccio and minestrone as regular features to allow more versatility and expedite things in the kitchen, Dottin explains.

All of the details, all of the changing arrangements are getting to DiPaolo.

"This is freaking me out! Every piece of this has all been stop and go. One thing affects the other. And yet, it's moving."

As if to demonstrate, she reaches into a folder and pulls out a business card. In black with gold lettering, it announces Ristorante DiPaolo.

January 17, 2006

The gold-on-black logo is emblazoned on the windows installed to look out on a cold, gray Avenue A.

Just inside the window, DiPaolo is meeting this morning with a woman who's come to talk about payroll services. DiPaolo's been waking up at 3 a.m. these increasingly crazy mornings and trying to drink less coffee.

After the payroll woman, she has to meet with a credit-card services vendor and then, with her son and Dottin, will move booths into the building so walls can be measured for sconces—then she meets with David Wiener of Great Lighting.

Meanwhile, the plumber's installing sinks, kitchen equipment will be arriving in the next few days, carpeting is scheduled for tomorrow, and a set of refinished Charlemont church pews are coming back from a Greenfield contractor the day after that.

"At this point, we're done with scheduling; all the stops are out. Whenever anyone can bring anything, we tell them to bring it. "We'll be working around each other the next two weeks."

The red oak flooring in the front part of the restaurant has two coats of polyurethane on it. The eight-foot tall divider doors with frosted glass are installed, framed so they're stationary rather than movable, as originally planned.

Without blueprints, she says, "Jim and I and sometimes Hilton have been weighing in, building it as we go. It's been a great lesson for me in letting go. I have a design in my mind, and then a guy comes by and says, 'You can't do that unless you throw in more money.'"

In his new kitchen, Dottin pantomimes how easy these white tile walls and tile floor will be to keep clean, how bright the lighting will be, how he'll be able to reach over to grab dishes and pans hanging overhead to swing back to the range and then to the counter where the waitstaff can pick up the ravioli or veal scallopini he's prepared.

"It's going to be great. I'm so excited," he says, eager to start cooking for real.

"The food comes out, the dishwashing junk goes in, the people just keep revolving," he says. "It's important to get a flow down, to get a circular motion."

Inspired by the primitive splash of colors she brought home in her Italy photo, DiPaolo shows pride in a wall she spent two days painting with three girlfriends. "This is my artwork," she declares.

With construction nearing an end and opening festivities already scheduled for February 10, DiPaolo says, "I'm starting to get nervous."

She's planning to interview a sous-chef next week but adds, "I'm not hiring anyone until I write a personnel policy and business strategy. It's very important to be clear about expectations about what the business represents, how you want people to perceive you and your service. That will be a work in progress."

DiPaolo has been told by the bank that she's going over budget in renovations and getting the business ready. "The truth will be known in about a week."

February 2, 2006

A gray-haired salesman is bending Dottin's ear near the bar as plumbers and carpenters walk by.

"We have hexagonal-shaped lobster ravioli. I could bring you product next week," he tells the chef, who's been at the work site all day with DiPaolo and an endless stream of workers and salesmen.

After DiPaolo's breakdown on the road Friday, Dottin, her son Nick and some friends hauled kitchen equipment as well as two cupboards, chairs, tables, and other items from the house and a rented Couture Brothers warehouse yesterday and over the weekend.

It took all of Friday for the rental company to send a mechanic and determine that the problem was caused by a frozen hydraulic mechanism and then tow in a new truck so the load could be transferred. The day was shot, DiPaolo said, and they ended truck swapping at 7:30 p.m.

It took a full day Saturday with seven adults helping to shuttle back and forth with two cupboards, tables, furniture, appliances, chairs, dishes and all the rest.

On Sunday, DiPaolo and a friend drove down to Ikea in West Haven, Connecticut and came back with a pair of stainless steel workbenches and faux wood wall cases to store wine, glasses, napkins, and such.

"Then, I couldn't stop myself," DiPaolo says, pointing to bags filled with tea lights, cups and other incidentals that looked too good to pass up.

"I'm ready to stop spending," she says. "We need to get the doors open. We're out of money. I had to borrow money from friends to pay the mortgage this month. The money's pouring out. We've already spent our entire equipment budget, so we're going to have to scramble."

At the same time, she knows, "We want our systems in place and want to do this right. It would be stupid to rush it now. But you get tired of carrying the load."

February 9, 2006

Across from the new entrance, a handwritten sentence on a flip chart spells out the basics of the embryonic restaurant for new employees:

"The customer is not always right, but regardless, our job is to make the customer feel that way."

It's the introductory page from a grounding session a few days ago for twenty-two would-be workers. Fed on bagels, cheese, fruit, and carrot cake, they're asked to leave their egos at the door of "a small, intimate business operation where nobody can run and hide."

With candles lit and table set in front of newly refinished pews, the enthused gathering of mostly seasoned restaurant workers is given a taste of what Ristorante DiPaolo will be like.

"This is not going to be high, high-end fine dining, but I want to it be a class act," DiPaolo says. "I want service to be key, and I want people to tag-team and back each other up."

There's plenty of elegance built into the space, from accent lighting beneath the bar to comfortable chairs in restrooms —yet there are also less obvious economies, like the twenty-nine-dollar mirror that replaced the one DiPaolo had her eye on, which had a jolting four-hundred-dollar price tag.

The electrical contractor wired the lights last weekend, followed Monday by the ventilation company, fire inspector, and workers connecting gas equipment. Fernandes and his crew are finishing up the four-month transformation of the space in preparation for friends helping with the final move of dishes, pots, pans, and racks from the house next weekend.

"Don't leave me, guys!" DiPaolo says in half jest as one contractor walks by. "I don't know what I'll do without you!"

Downstairs, beyond the walk-in cooler and the start of a dry storage area, her newly lit, bare office has its first piece of furniture flush against the wall: an old wooden library desk sawed in half and delivered by her ex-husband.

"It's very surreal," she says of her long journey. "At the same time, it's about time. It feels like it was meant to be, and I really feel blessed."

Excited to see the long-vacant space coming alive, plenty of people have been looking in the windows of former Laundromat/Creamee. The former community organizer thinks this might give added momentum for invigorating downtown.

"I hope it inspires people in the very least to shift their thinking from a doom-and-gloom mentality. It's just a subtle shift to realize that it's really possible to have what we want."

In the past year or two, she's watched restaurants come and go and has seen the upheaval after the Shady Glen up the street changed hands.

"It's scary," she says. "I'm going to have to draw people in and be a destination location. On the one hand, it makes me a little nervous. On the other, I think there are a lot of us who are looking for good places to eat and hang out."

March 3, 2006

A jazzy version of the 1937 Duke Ellington hit "Caravan" pulsates from ceiling speakers in a space thoroughly transformed with lamps installed over the bar and ceiling fans slowly turning.

"We're down to the little, nitty-gritty stuff," says DiPaolo, who's losing patience as things come together uneasily two weeks before opening. "Yesterday, I was absolutely crazy," she says, pointing to a red fire detector a contractor installed directly over a front-room table when she wasn't looking.

"It's like a sore thumb in your eye," she says. "It makes me sick to my stomach. I called them up today, and he said, 'Why does it matter where it is?' But they're going to move it. I'm starting to get frantic. I just don't see how it's going to come together."

When the electrician showed up—a day late—he refused to climb on the roof to switch wires for the exhaust fan, which was spinning the wrong way. She also needs the plumber to come back to help set up the espresso machine and soda gun. And Coca-Cola has refused to service her, saying her projected volume of customers didn't warrant a contract. So, she's turned to Pepsi.

Meanwhile, she has to get data on her new employees to the Buckland women who will be handling her payroll, she's got to get the fax machine to work, and the phone line has to be reinstalled so the cordless phone now connected in the cellar can be in range upstairs. The office computer isn't hooked up to the Internet, and the point-of-sale cash register needs wine and liquor prices programmed in. The flurry of loose details is maddening.

In the space of a few minutes, Larry Clark from the Music Store comes in to check on how the new sound system is working, and the refrigeration technician, who's fixing equipment in the kitchen, announces he's going to replace some of the brittle wires that have been causing malfunctions.

"Yay!!!" she shouts. Having refrigerators working properly is key to the food ordering she has to do next week.

Like an overdue expectant mother tired of answering everyone's questions about whether she's given birth yet, DiPaolo says, "It's a pain, and it's testing my patience.

"People keep saying, 'What's taking you so long?' It's been four months, and I've totally renovated and transformed a near condemned building. It's a thousand things: if the electrician doesn't show up, that impacts the carpentry and anything else. That happens constantly."

On top of that, she says, "The money's all dried up. We went forty thousand dollars over budget, and I'm trying to find an extra forty thousand dollars right now."

She has a separate pool of money specifically for startup and working capital she's not touching yet.

"Hilton went to Kittredge yesterday" and returned from the Springfield supplier with storage containers, spoons, pans, and gadgets that he needed. "When he came back, he looked like a kid on Christmas morning just back from a candy shop."

"This is it," says DiPaolo. "We've got to do it. Hopefully folks will be forgiving in the beginning as we practice."

March 4, 2006

The parking lot is full and the lights are on at 4 p.m. A woman appears expectantly at the front door to ask if the restaurant is open.

It's only a wine-tasting, though. Five servers are assembled at the gold-speckled bar, where bottles of wine are displayed with stickies listing their prices: twenty dollars, twenty-six dollars, forty dollars.

Servers Gretchen Bennett, formerly of the Blue Heron, Kat Walker of the People's Pint, Adora LaRoche of Peterborough's Aqua Bistro, and Jonathan Wood sit around the bar. DiPaolo turns off Marvin Gaye's 1967 hit "I Heard It through the Grapevine" on the stereo.

They sample each of the wines, beginning with a Chardonnay, one of two whites. They start by sniffing wines still in bottles and swirling glasses.

DiPaolo asks for descriptive adjectives and explains, "I just want you to get familiar with the taste so you can sell it."

"Apple citrusy, but mild," says Bennett, "Clean, soft. It would be good with shellfish or fish."

"This is a keeper," says Bennett of the Chardonnay, as DiPaolo moves on to the Principessa Perlante, an aperitif in a shapely bottle marked twenty-six dollars. Dottin pops in from the kitchen and translates the name as "the Princess speaks," which sets off jokes about it referring to DiPaolo.

It's a sparkling wine described as crisp without much flavor. Though it's one of five Italian wines that survived from an earlier tasting of some seventy wines, DiPaolo says, "We don't have to have this. This might be good in dead of summer out on the patio."

DiPaolo mentions that yesterday, she and Dottin sampled organic beef and pork that they're going to offer on the menu. "It was out of this world. They slaughter and pack it in New York, and we get it the next day."

As she begins pouring a Chianti Classico, Dottin brings out bread in metal bowls along with olive oil for dipping. They've been searching for a good bread as far as Cambridge, and they've happily settled on something from Bread Euphoria from Williamsburg. Then, the chef brings out casserole dishes of manicotti Florentine, which the servers sample along with the bread and "velvety" Chianti, oohing and ahhing over each.

March 15, 2006

With one day to go before an afternoon reception and two days before the soft opening, Ristorante DiPaolo is bustling.

A set of large cast-iron chandeliers, just in from the blacksmith and waiting for the electrician, aren't centered the way she wanted, but they'll have to do.

Four colorful paintings, each four by four feet, look like they were created for the harvest gold and claret walls. In fact, a friend of DiPaolo arranged for them to come out of storage, where Shelburne painter Bonnie Griffith had left them before moving out of the area.

"It's absolutely perfect for this space," she exclaims. "I'm really excited."

A hostess station that had been a lectern at Saint Anne's Church waits for the first guests to arrive. Pastry chef Suzanne Hynes, who's taken this job while waiting for her restaurant Bottle of Bread to re-open, is preparing a chocolate mousse terrine. It will be on the menu along with tiramisu, Crème Brûlée and biscotti. For Friday with about fifty guests expected, she's prepared hand-rolled truffles, cheesecake, and almond frangipane tart.

Sous-chef Aaron Fides, who's come to work from The Deerfield Inn, carries an armful of bread in the kitchen. "Making croutons, baby!"

Dottin explains there won't be specials on the menu for a while. "Everything's going to be special!"

March 16, 2006

"I'm overcome with joy," DiPaolo says when she's stopped racing around the extreme makeover at 166 Avenue A to reposition bouquets around the restaurant and snuff out excess candles in order to enhance the subtle effect of the lighting fixtures.

Dottin, pen and meat thermometer stuffed into the arm pocket of his gleaming chef's uniform, carries a large platter of antipasto into the front room where cushiony chairs and faux leather banquettes await bankers and town officials.

"This is intense," says Dottin, who's been here since this morning in preparation for the 5 p.m. reception that's minutes away. "At least in the very beginning until you catch up with the rhythm."

Guests begin arriving from Greenfield Co-Operative Bank, from the Franklin County Community Development Corporation where DiPaolo used to work, from Franklin County Housing and Redevelopment Authority along with Montague selectmen Al Ross and Patty Pruitt and other town officials.

Town Planner Robin Sherman, standing near a chafing dish filled with farfalle pasta, Pekarski's sausage, and meatballs from DiPaolo's own recipe, says this is just the latest manifestation of a blossoming downtown and a textbook case of sweat equity and how public dollars can spark private initiative.

"This is the culmination of twenty-five years of work redeveloping Turners Falls. We've always had a vision that the cultural, historical, and natural resources were assets that could bring people here. This is a perfect example how we see the town developing. Because of its cultural and natural resources, people are coming. Now they have a place to eat."

DiPaolo's longtime friend, Kate Douglas, greets her: "You've transformed this place!"

"A little bit," jokes DiPaolo after nearly three hundred thousand dollars in renovations. She adds, "It's everything I've dreamed about."

Italy's Amalfi Coast offers inspiration on the April calendar hung in the wait station as servers Wood and LaRoche punch orders into the computerized register and check with chef Dottin on the specials this Wednesday: grilled tuna with roasted red pepper, Julienne vegetables, and scallion sauce plus New York strip steak with baked potatoes.

Six of the restaurant's burners are fired up under broth-filled stock pots, a quartered pasta pot, and pans as the restaurant opens at 5 p.m. with two reservations in hand.

Dottin and line-chef Fides, in contrasting black and white caps, master a swirl of sautée pans in a culinary ballet accompanied by the roar of the overhead vent roar, the loud hum of the convection oven, and Latin background music. It's coming from the stereo system in the front of the house, where DiPaolo is greeting walk-ins to what by 5:30 has grown to be a half dozen tables of diners.

Back and forth—Dottin adding a pinch of Spanish saffron from a tin to the frutti de Mar and Fides removing stuffed chicken breasts from the oven—the kitchen partners dance past one another with little instruction.

On the other side of the equipment, salad chef Carmen Sibrian quietly cuts up carrots and onions, adding them to pre-washed spinach and greens from Seeds of Solidarity Farm in Orange.

"It's like a piece of art," Dottin says as he arranges scallops, mussels and calamari on a bed of risotto. "You make it look nice. You make it taste good."

April 7, 2006

On the other side of her dream realized, DiPaolo is still swimming in a sea of details as she gets down to her morning's work at 10:30 on a Friday three weeks after opening.

Upstairs, dessert chef Hynes is preparing chocolate mousse and cheesecake crust, and a Thurston Foods truck is delivering cartons of goods for the weekend ahead. Downstairs, in her fluorescent lit office, DiPaolo is looking at a long white wall of stickies surrounded by invoices and a dozen labeled loose-leaf binders: menus and recipes, beverage and soda accounts, desserts.

There's also a small bottle of homeopathic sleeping pills for DiPaolo, who is finding it hard to wind down to sleep after a busy night's work.

"Every minute is packed solid," she says. "You just go."

She juggles her hands up and down slowly as she describes a jumble of emotions. "One minute, I'm happy buying flowers and making arrangements, and the next minute, I've got staff coming at me with scheduling issues and the rug's already soiled and how do we stay organized?"

Things are wild but going wildly well.

"The first week was horrendous. It was impossible for one person to juggle," she says. "I'm incredibly blessed with many girlfriends who have many talents, and I just called in the ranks. We were so slammed and overwhelmed that I walked in the kitchen for something and there was one of my girlfriends doing dishes. I didn't even know she'd come in."

In addition to dishwasher and computer-register headaches, there was a sense all the carnival rides had started full tilt and were nearly out of control.

"The money's a scary thing, because you know you need help. But how are you going to pay them?" says DiPaolo, who has friends coming in to help with the payroll for her nineteen paid workers with the myriad notes saying who's come to work which hours for which job at which rate.

"My ultimate goal is to find a system for every paper and clip," she says. "Til I get a home for everything, a sign for everything, I'm not going to rest."

Delivery men and visitors interrupt DiPaolo even now, six hours before the restaurant opens, and the phone rings constantly.

"I've been so inundated with phone messages," she says "I'm checking messages after closing at 11, 11:30. Last night, I had 14 phone messages. You can't call people back at that time, so that's what I do first thing in the morning."

By then, it's too late, though, for some people who have been trying since 5 p.m. to make that night's reservations. One couple showed up last night really upset because she hadn't phoned them back. Although DiPaolo finally calmed them down with a quiet table, the customer warned her, "We'll forgive you this time because you're new, but don't let it happen again."

She promises, "I'm trying to get better."

Ristorante DiPaolo has been quiet on Monday evenings, a welcome respite for now—and a little slow on Wednesdays. But by word-of-mouth, it's been busy with people mostly from surrounding towns on Thursdays and packed on the weekends. DiPaolo says she's now turning tables over one and a half times and is full in the early evenings. Tuesdays, when the business is closed, she spends all day taking care of payroll, invoices and other details while the space upstairs is cleaned for another week.

As she tweaks details and tries to better organize systems and staff, DiPaolo says the treadmill she's on seems to be getting her somewhere. For one thing, money is beginning to flow in, so she's no longer living off credit cards and trying to figure new ways to shuffle money.

"It was very scary the last two weeks before we opened," she admits. "We're not making a profit yet, but we're paying the bills. That's a good thing. But now we have to keep this pace up in order to eventually make a profit. We have to keep generating business."

Asked if that's a scary notion, she nods several times before she voices, "Yeah."

But she's already beginning to look into building a patio and launching a luncheon menu of salads, kabobs, and panini sandwiches for this summer to fill a need she sees in a community that's beginning to attract professional workers and out-of-town visitors.

"I'm in a high learning curve," she says after just a few weeks in business, "but I'm starting to feel less frantic personally. It's all going to smooth out."

Along with reading the body language of customers and feeling her way through how many servers, expediters, busboys, and bartenders to schedule, DiPaolo has found a pork and a veal item under-priced and nudged it up by a couple of dollars, and Dottin wants to remove a couple of dishes that aren't big sellers.

But for the most part, she adds, "People are cleaning their plates. We're throwing no food away. It's so gratifying. It feels like I've invited people into my home, and they leave full and happy. And most of them say, 'We'll be back.'"

❈ ❈ ❈

Ristorante DiPaolo closed after nearly seven years.

Jean-Claude van Itallie, playwright

A Centered Life on the Edge

August 13, 1998

*Responding to the advice I'd received soon after moving
to Franklin County, that "there's a story behind every tree,"
I interviewed legendary playwright Jean-Claude van Itallie
several times at his home in Rowe, in the region's far
northwestern corner. Later, his theater training center burned in
a January 2000 fire. When he died in 2021, his New York Times
obituary called him "a mainstay of the experimental theater."*

❖ ❖ ❖

Standing beam-like at the heart of a three-story barn, Jean-Claude
van Itallie directs a crew of contractors on exactly where and how he
wants a bathroom and closet located.

Sporting a pink T-shirt and jeans with dark blue baseball cap
covering wispy white hair, the balding sixty-two-year-old van Itallie

is shorter and slighter than the four workers with whom he pores over a blueprint.

After thirty years of restoration efforts, this Rowe barn represents perhaps the most elaborate—and certainly the most structural—of this playwright-director-teacher-actor's lifetime of works. An interior silo, for example, will house a meditation room gazing over a nearby field.

Van Itallie's attention is riveted at the moment on this Davenport Road barn-turned-teaching studio. But he's looking ahead, too, to a series of other stellar projects: tonight's Boston opening program by Pilgrim Theater of his retelling of *The Tibetan Book of the Dead for Reading Aloud. The Playwright's Workbook,* his collection of 13 workshops, was published last year.

Van Itallie will also launch a series of West Coast workshops next winter and then tour California with his autobiographical performance piece, *War, Sex, Singing, and Dancing.*

Van Itallie's life began at the torturous center of what was stirring in 1930s Europe and moved on to the heart of the theater's rebirth in Greenwich Village in the 1960s.

Through it all, he has mastered "living on the edge"—as a radical playwright, a Jew, a homosexual and for seventeen years a vegan. He has spent decades centering his mind and soul through Buddhism, through meditation, through physical workouts.

He fondly recalls life in "the Village" in the sixties.

"I was very lucky to be in the right place at the right time," says van Itallie, seated on the front porch of the farmhouse his family bought in 1955. "There was the sense of being at the center of a creative whirlpool."

The porch—where he relaxes and reflects, eyes closed Buddha-like, and focuses on his past and his thoughts—is adorned with a gilded Asian amulet, a cast-iron bell, and mirror. Just above van Itallie's head is perched a nest where a swallow also seems at peace.

In contrast to mainstream theater, which deals with "merely the psychological spectrum (and) . . . wasn't having us," radical dramatists like van Itallie expressed politics, philosophy, and poetry using unconventional approaches.

Van Itallie emigrated with his family from Belgium at age four, the same year as Nazis invaded Brussels. He grew up in suburban New York and turned to theater in reaction to the world of his father, an investment banker.

"I found that the whole grownup world was not playful enough. It horrified me, and I felt like I would be in a straitjacket all my life. I went in the completely opposite direction."

Theater, which took hold of him as a young Harvard student, "was like many things in my life—something I found myself doing: directing, acting, writing plays. It was the most fun thing in my life at the time."

The off-Broadway Open Theater, for which van Itallie became resident writer in 1963, was on the cutting edge of innovation without scenery, costumes, or makeup. He brought the troupe to the Rowe farm to work on plays.

"In one week, I wrote three plays to perform here, on that hill," he recalls with a glow, pointing.

Van Itallie captured international attention for *The Serpent,* which explored "the myths that moved us, from Adam and Eve to the Kennedy assassination." That play, the culmination of his collaboration with Open Theater, was first produced in Rome.

His landmark, *America Hurrah,* which ran 634 performances off Broadway from 1966 to 1968, represented van Itallie's attempt to try his hand writing a commercial play.

"It was the first attempt of the Village scene to get the attention of the world," he recalls. "We thought it would be a commercial flop. We thought the critics would hate it because of what it said politically and because of the unusual form, as three short plays."

Instead, critics like Walter Kerr of the *New York Times* called it, "A whisper in the wind." A hit, it went on to London, and van Itallie's delight turned to fear of being overly embraced by the Establishment: "How can it be that they're liking our protest?"

If the play was a sellout, though, van Itallie didn't feel it was he who had sold out.

"I made absolutely no compromise in the play," he declares.

With his parents and friends putting up the seventeen thousand dollars in production costs—a pittance by today's standards—he felt few demands to tinker with his work.

Today, the playwright looks back proudly on *Motel,* one of the plays within his trio of one-acts, *America Hurrah,* because it openly expresses his anger at feeling repressed politically and personally. Using papier-mâché dolls, one of which becomes decapitated on stage, the work bonds its author with audiences, who embraced it.

If van Itallie had begun work in theater in a different era, he muses, "I think I would have been less radical in my form. I would have found ways to corrupt the existing forms more subtly."

He went on to write versions of four major Chekhov plays. His *Uncle Vanya* was produced at Broadway's Circle-in-the-Square Theater in 1965 starring Tom Courtenay, and *The Cherry Orchard* was staged at Lincoln Center with Irene Worth, Raul Julia, and Meryl Streep.

Chekhov, whose works van Itallie rewrote in English using someone else's direct translations, "became one of my teachers." These versions are still used in colleges around the country, he says.

Rather than a commercial career in New York, "I decided I wanted to work on my soul and spirit. That involved sacrifice."

He turned to Buddhist meditation and veganism. And truly moved to Rowe, where he'd been living six months of the year since the late sixties. Though he now spends from nine to ten months a year here, he maintains a Manhattan apartment and says he doesn't feel isolated.

"I consider myself blessed to be up here. Every day, I thank God I'm here. I've had enough cultural stimulation to last a lifetime. People raised in rural areas may rightly ask themselves, 'Who needs it? We have nature.'"

New York living, however, "takes all the energy you have just to breathe. Who has energy to create art?"

Now with the Shantigar workshop barn taking shape—he refuses to pressure himself with schedule but hopes it will be ready this winter—"the world will be coming to me."

Van Itallie plans for Shantigar, Tibetan for "peaceful home", to be "a place where artistic and spiritual practices meet."

Rather than a performance space, Shantigar is intended to provide a place for actors and non-actors alike to learn theater techniques through meditation, movement, and other spiritual practices and performance techniques.

The fifteen workshops that van Itallie already has conducted over the past three summers in Rowe have attracted teachers, actors, and even corporate participants honing their communication skills.

Van Itallie, whose parents bought the Davenport Road farm seven months before Yankee Atomic purchased the site of what was to become New England's first commercial reactor, has also been an active founding member of the anti-nuclear Citizens Awareness Network.

"For me, it all is political," he says, speaking of theater as well as life. "If you go deeply enough into yourself and come up with deeply personal stuff, it turns out that's what you share with other people."

The Holocaust, which cost the lives of several members of his family, left van Itallie haunted by a profound fear and "continually looking for a safe haven," he says. The Nazi onslaught is the subject of several of his works, including *Paradise Ghetto*.

Growing up speaking English and French at home, "I learned that reality is not contained in any single language. It led to my fascination with words and to my becoming a writer."

From a young age, van Itallie had learned another crucial lesson:

"Being an exile, a Jew, a gay man, for seventeen years a vegan, living unpartnered in the country, I've learned to live on the edge. That's a great strength."

Van Itallie came out to his parents as a homosexual forty years ago.

"I was working in the theater, living in Greenwich Village . . . it wasn't such a big deal to me. I wasn't living in a world where I felt I was risking so much."

In *War, Sex, Singing and Dancing*, which premiered in Shelburne Falls in May, and which he'll present at New York's LaMama Theater next March, van Itallie bares his soul: fleeing Holocaust Europe, dealing with fame, being gay.

"It's a miracle I didn't die of AIDS, as so many of my friends did. I escaped it. I escaped the Holocaust. It's a survivor's responsibility to tell about it the best way he can."

Despite his thirty-five-year career in the theater, writing more than thirty plays and screenplays as well as teaching playwriting at Princeton, Columbia, and Middlebury as well as a host of other campuses, van Itallie did not face the audience directly as an actor until 1996 in the collaborative work, *Guys Dreamin'*.

"Acting takes a lot of courage," he says. "I've been preparing for it all my life. I was frightened by it, but I had to put my body where my mouth is. Performing finally was inevitable."

Van Itallie sees stage fright as a test. Surmounting it "is like a rehearsal for dying."

Exposing his inner life on stage, as he does in *War, Sex, Singing, and Dancing*, may be an even more courageous act.

"I guess I'm a risk taker," he says. "I'm standing out there and being as personally whole as I can be. I bring everything I have to bear, not only letting it hang out, but waving it; not only not hiding behind the word, but speaking it; not only speaking it, but singing it."

He pauses, then adds, "Isn't it weird that it's taken as long as it has, after doing this a lifetime?"

❊ ❊ ❊

Jean-Claude van Itallie died on September 9, 2021.

Paula Green, peacebuilder

Lowering the Temperature

May 22, 2021

This post-retirement article grew out of my deep concerns about the frightening political and social polarization in this country and my curiosity about the lessons from other nations that had recently experienced civil war. Paula Green, whose profile as a peacebuilder appears in my book Good Will & Ice Cream, *had emphasized parallels with her work through the nonprofit Karuna Center for Peacebuilding she'd founded. Also, Karuna ran a series at the time exploring threats to our democracy as presaged elsewhere.*

❋ ❋ ❋

When she retired in June 2015 from decades of traveling to war-torn parts of the globe and training peacemakers to lead discussions of what survivors of violent conflicts had endured and how to begin their healing, Paula Green had already begun seeing our nation's fabric fraying.

Yet Green never expected to see the crying need at home for work she'd done in Bosnia, Rwanda, Nigeria, and elsewhere as Karuna Center for Peacebuilding's founding director.

The Hands Across the Hills effort that drew Green and other Leverett residents to eastern Kentucky to explore social and political differences after the 2016 election has received national and international media attention as an example of the need to bridge the growing US political divide.

But heightened political violence—most notably the January 6, 2021 attack on the US Capitol—has led Karuna to launch an online discussion series examining lessons from its partners around the world —lessons that can be applied to deepening political polarization here.

"We're trying to translate that model of partnering with organizations to bring the dialogue and trauma-healing work we've done overseas to address what's needed here," says Karuna Center Executive Director Polly Byers about the organization's Bridging Community Across Divides series of "lessons from far and near."

With four online discussions already presented and more planned, the series tries to "highlight creative, innovative, and successful responses to conflict that are building community and supporting lasting peace." The first of its programs, The Power of Dialogue, featured Hands Across the Hills co-facilitators Green and Ben Fink discussing the in-depth conversations between the Leverett and Kentucky contingents.

Rather than trying to change voting behavior or opinions, Green explains, the process is about working to understand a culture that votes so differently on guns, abortion, immigration, and other issues.

"Is this all emotional? Are you avoiding the issues?" attendees asked Green, who responded when eleven Kentuckians first visited in October 2017.

Green brought up the issue of guns.

"What makes you feel safe?" she asked. She found that her Leverett neighbors felt safe when nobody has guns around them, while the Kentucky visitors responded that they feel safe when everyone has guns.

"We talked about the opioid crisis, and the Kentuckians said people are robbing grandmothers' televisions to sell for money to buy opioids, and they felt they needed guns to protect grandmothers. We went at this very hard issue in a way that we could hear each other.

We want to go underneath, to get to the life experience that gets you to why you want to vote for Trump, what makes you want guns?"

In the second gathering a month later, Tim Phillips of Boston-based Beyond Conflict described that organization's decades of work, beginning after the Cold War as Eastern European leaders sought guidance in preparing for societal change.

Around 2015, Phillips began hearing from peacemakers in other countries who advised, "You need to focus on your own country."

"Like canaries in a coal mine, they could see and sense the deepening divide in the US," he said.

Brain science research, he learned, was uncovering an underlying behavioral basis for the work he'd been doing in conflict resolution.

"It's tough to negotiate with a humiliated partner," he heard from one workshop participant from Northern Ireland. Then a brain and behavioral scientist awakened him to the relevance of new research that shows why so many conflicts and peace agreements seem so intractable.

Instead of rational beings, Phillips said, "We're emotionally based beings who can only think rationally when we feel that our identities, as we see ourselves, are understood and valued by others."

Research on the psychology of polarization that Beyond Conflict has done with the University of Pennsylvania shows that once interactions go from profound disagreement to us versus them, "a whole range of unconscious psychological processes kick in that serve to drive us further apart," Philips explained. Unconsciously, the psychology of polarization tends to exaggerate how much the other group might disrespect or dehumanize you.

"The more separated we are, the less contact we have, the more we're getting our news from our various social media channels or we don't live next to each other or we don't go to the same schools or churches together, we don't play the same sports. We start basing our views of each other on these silos."

As a result, the research shows, "Polarization is becoming more toxic, like a public health threat," he added.

That same gathering's discussion—where Nigerian psychologist Dr. Fatima Akilu of Neem Foundation explained her organization's post-trauma work with victims and perpetrators of political violence—can be viewed at karunacenter.org/ building-community.

Karuna Center's series also included a conversation about lessons learned from working on reconciliation in the aftermath of 1994 Rwandan and 1992-1995 Bosnian conflicts. Another discussion, three weeks later, brought together participants in a Mediators Without Borders network of community-based monitors, educators, and responders to build cohesion and negotiate conflicts as they might develop around this country. The non-partisan, volunteer TRUST Network, established by a consortium of organizations as tensions over US elections intensified last September, is based on the America's Peacemakers initiative of the US Justice Department under the 1964 Civil Rights Act to help communities facing discrimination disputes.

Green's own anxiety began as the 2016 elections started heating up "because I had seen in so many war-torn countries where the roots of war were connected to the dehumanization of 'the other.' I had a worrying sense of the dehumanization and blame, and the aggression that comes along with that, was escalating."

The growing verbal attacks on Muslims, Mexicans and others that Green and collaborating peace workers heard "became more alarming," especially given her work in Rwanda. There, intertribal tensions where the Hutu-led government in the early 1990s called the minority Tutsi tribe "cockroaches" led to the 1994 genocide, resulting in nearly a million deaths.

"When a human population is reduced to a bug, you can kill them," says Green. Like with Nazi characterization of Jews as rats, "It's classic example of dehumanization. Everybody in Rwanda had a transistor radio, which blasted antagonisms and stimulated violence."

Around the same time, Yugoslavia's interwoven Serbian, Croatian, and Bosnian society was torn apart after the 1980 death of President Josip Broz Tito, with Slobadan Milosovic resurrecting a six-hundred-year-old humiliating incident as a battle cry that led to atrocities against Bosnian Muslims, including genocide.

"Yugoslavia was a united country under Tito," Green says. "Before the war, people intermarried without even asking the origin of the family. Nobody cared. Religion was not about anything very serious for the people. It was an identity, but it was muted. Everybody looked alike. They spoke the same language."

In both those violent conflicts and others where Green worked with peacemakers on the ground, "It only takes one manipulative, strong leader in power to stoke those grievances."

❂ ❂ ❂

A "tremendous insight" for Green and other Hands Across the Hills participants, she says, is this: "A person is larger than their vote.

People I disagree with have full biographies in the way they've been shaped and understand the world. There's always a back story, and if I remind myself of that, it stops me from demonizing others in my own mind and helps me see them in their fullness. It makes me realize they, in their fullness, need respect just as I need it. To discover a whole person under a vote is a lovely thing. All beings are complex and have full lives. We're shaped by enormous social forces that tell us a lot about ourselves."

Karuna's new series is part of an effort by the organization to focus on domestic as well as international peace-building issues. Building Community Across Divides follows a series of discussions and workshops last year about past and present native communities in the Connecticut River Valley as well as a 2017 lecture series on Transforming this Moment: Bridging Our Divides.

It's unclear, Byers says, exactly where the current online series of conversations will lead. The federal Department of Homeland Security has stepped up its funding to respond to domestic terrorism threats with a program aimed at supporting "diverse, innovative, and community-driven methods to prevent domestic terrorism while respecting civil rights and liberties."

In the March 10 discussion, Mirsad "Miki" Jacevic, Karuna's senior peacebuilding advisor, asked, "How do we do Karuna-like work across America?

"My slight apprehension and hope for the US is how do we make this work relevant to the people, so this is not something 'out there.' It's very much historically needed in this country. How do we indeed stop this great tendency of American people to say, 'Let's focus on the future, forget about the past.' There are many historical wounds in this country that are never even opened, let alone discussed. How do we really keep at this?"

"We try not to talk to anybody about anything important," Green says. "That lays the seeds for more violence, for more alienation."

※ ※ ※

Paula Green died on February 21, 2023.

Kevin Ford shears a somewhat reluctant sheep.

Shear Simplicity

May 7, 2016

Much of the joy I derive from living where I do comes from the wealth of small-scale agriculture that endures because of hard work by farmers and supporting groups promoting local products. I'd already done stories on Mark Duprey's sheep farm, featured in my book Inner Landscapes. *When he told me about an upcoming day of shearing by Kevin Ford, I was eager to experience and write about it.*

❀ ❀ ❀

There's a wary and downright woolly crowd waiting for the moment to get clipped.

Every five minutes or so, a worker reaches into the bungee-held ante-pen of about thirty white and black-faced sheep and randomly chooses one from the cross-bred flock. The animal is escorted out by one hand grabbing onto some hind-section wool and another gently pulling back on the head to force the sheep backward.

Only about half of the sheep, falling back onto their rumps and then scooted backward into place by forelegs, will get a "brush cut" as part of the annual shearing ritual at Leyden Glen Farm.

Escorted out of the pen by white-haired, bearded Kevin Ford of Charlemont, the others get a traditional blade cut.

This is no ordinary fleecing. Yet, it's the way shearing has been done for centuries, and the seventy-year-old master blade shearer is thought to be one of the only professional shearers exclusively using the traditional technique in the United States.

It is less dazzling than *Edward Scissorhands*. It's more like *Dances with Woolies*.

Ford's left hand, and each of his other limbs including elbows and knees, are used to keep sheep in place—and relaxed. But, in his right hand, he wields a pair of British-made, spring-loaded shears with 7 1/4-inch blades. About five minutes later, the sheep scampers from his makeshift baa-baa chair naked of that woolly winter coat.

Ford literally wrote the book *Shearing Day: Sheep Handling Wool Science and Shearing with Blades* on blade shearing. He also writes the "Shearing Notes" column in *Sheep* magazine, which refers to him as "America's foremost 'blade' (hand) sheepshearer."

In addition to traveling each winter to shear in North Carolina, Virginia, Maryland, and Delaware as well as shearing around the Northeast, the tall, slender shearing pro has led workshops and demonstrations in his traditional skill in Maine, North Carolina, and elsewhere for young farmers to learn the craft.

Here at Mark Duprey and Kristin Nicholas's Leyden Glen Farm—although the "here" is really inside an open-air barn off one of its Bernardston fields—Ford has been shearing the flocks for about twenty-five years.

It's more important to Duprey that a shearer "shows up when he says he's going to show up"—not that he uses super sharp blade shears or an electric implement. The farmer guesses it probably makes little difference to the sheep, either. But as practical as the farmer is, he admits there's something "very peaceful" about Ford's steady hand snipping, where "all you're hearing is just the clicking of the shears."

Because there are 130 or so sheep—mostly from 2 to 4 years old—getting sheared today with another 100 or so planned on a second day, Ford is joined by another contract shearer, Gwen Hinman from Ackworth, New Hampshire. Unlike Ford, the 41-year-old professional shearer—one of about two dozen in New England, she guesses—uses electric shears hooked to a power source hanging from the ceiling of the open-air barn.

So there are actually two baa-baa chairs.

Although most of the sheep, weighing an average of maybe 150 pounds, outweigh her, Hinman has little trouble wrestling each out of the pen. It does seem a little harder than it used to be, though, she says.

Holding firmly onto the animal's rear and head, she backs each sheep onto the plywood sheet placed on the soil. There, she positions and repositions each animal, buzzing down each side, under its limbs and around its head, down its back. All the while, the sheep squirms as she firmly moves the animal's front right leg behind her own right leg. Or whatever works.

Hinman works by using her knee here, her leg there with her free hand to hold the sheep's ear, limb, or a clump of fleece strategically.

Suddenly, she has the lamb's two front hooves gingerly held behind her arm.

"Some of them are just easy. Some of them are miserable," observes Duprey as one of the cheviots—a wilder breed of sheep that he favors for its toughness—fusses with Ford as he tries to keep the ewe steady on his plywood shearing board like a toddler getting a rare haircut.

It takes obvious strength and agility to assure that Hinman and Ford are in control, minimizing the animal's attempts to get out of these awkward positions.

"Would you mind doing a ram?" asks Duprey before bringing over a waist-high Dorset for Hinman to shear. The farmer pulls the animal's rear legs down to get it in place. It's one of six rams on a four-hundred-animal sheep farm where just one sheep—a black one that used to be his daughter's pet lamb—has a name: Cora.

With sixteen years of experience, Hinman, whose father taught her to shear, can get the fleece gracefully uncloaked from the animal in one seamless robe. That's so the fleece can be washed and carded efficiently for sale at the best price. It is the New Zealand shearing technique, where the sheep seems almost magically to disrobe to reveal a lighter skin underneath.

Yet, the fleece is not always as white as snow. Newly revealed grayish patches on the underside of the fleece are dirty spots where the animal may have been rubbing against some filth or even have had a lamb hopping on its back, Hinman explains.

With the fleece lying at her feet, the shearer releases the sheep to run off to join the rest of the newly shorn flock in the field.

And it's on to the next, as twenty-four-year-old farm worker Rachel Haas, a recent Hampshire College graduate who lives in Montague, helps stuff the fleece into a clean plastic bag set up on a hanging frame just outside the barn. By the time they're done, six or seven of the bags will be stuffed, each with roughly two hundred pounds of wool.

Duprey, 58, thinks back to the shearing workshop he took while a student at Stockbridge School of Agriculture, where he learned he'd gladly pay somebody else to shear for him.

The shearer's skill may look effortless, yet it's exhausting—even just to watch. The shearer will wrestle and then completely bend over a squirming animal without inflicting injury or pain, maneuvering the sheep constantly not only to make the next section of wool accessible to the shears, but to keep the critter from getting bored and antsy.

On his feet, Ford wears shearer's sole-less moccasins, professional footwear from New Zealand that keeps feet low to the ground and anchored for better control of the sheep.

"You control the sheep with your feet, a lot of it," explains Hinman, "so you can feel what's happening. If they're in one position too long, they get impatient. So if you keep them moving, it sort of relaxes them."

Dorset mixed-breed sheep do appear relaxed, almost mesmerized as they begin to lose their wooly coat, despite an occasional jostling from a rambunctious ram or ewe.

"Positioning the sheep and the shears is really a basic skill of shearing," observes Ford, whose voice is as calm as some of the animals. "It's about moving the animal through those positions so the area of the body you're shearing is convenient, and the sheep is passive due to realizing it's being well-handled."

He pauses thoughtfully for a minute.

"The sheep's kept at a big disadvantage. The sheep is pretty much convinced that struggling to get away is futile, so it waits for a better opportunity. Its sense is that the shears are not tense, and it's not a threatening situation."

The chorus of bleating is almost constant, though it shifts from one side of the barn to another, from one animal to another, from high pitch to low pitch to a very loud low pitch as a lamb bleats here, a ewe there, and suddenly from an already-shorn sheep that's popped its head back into the barn to see what's going down. Adding to the fun is an occasional sheep wandering back into the barn or one of the lambs mixed in the pen slipping out—maybe searching for its mother?—and then out beyond the shearing area to join the shorn flock outdoors.

Border Collie Kate waits nearby, of course, ever eager to help if humans would allow.

☒ ☒ ☒

Ford, who grew up in Newton, Massachusetts, took a fancy to sheep while visiting cousins in Galway, Ireland, in 1975.

It was there—where farmers generally shear their own flocks of maybe twenty or thirty sheep—that he first took to blade-shearing, learning techniques that fathers generally teach their sons—or, as with Hinman, their daughters—as part of general farm trade.

"That's where I got my start," recalls Ford, who in 1991 took a shearing workshop in Putney, Vermont, with an instructor from New Zealand and showed up with his blades. The workshop leader was a good friend and neighbor of Peter Burnett, chief blade shearing instructor in that country of three million people and sixty million sheep.

"When I got to New Zealand, they brought me over to Peter's house and took me to my first shearing shed," the kind of big barn fully equipped for shearing that's part of every large sheep farm in New Zealand.

Ford began shearing with the intention of eventually getting his own flock but instead came to enjoy the life of a full-time, itinerant shearer. In the 1980s, he moved to Shelburne Falls and a couple of years later settled down on Warner Hill in Charlemont.

"I never did buy a farm. It was a lot easier to get involved by shearing, just by shearing," he says while taking a rare midday break.

He favors the simplicity of hand shearing, which he considers "a bit more athletic" but no more virtuosic than using electric shears or clippers.

"It's independent from needing a power source, so it's very handy for a small flock. You can go anywhere the sheep are. Just get 'em into a pen, and it's very quick to set up."

With an almost hypnotic click-click-click of his Sheffield English blades held together by a single arc of a spring, Ford enjoys the quiet traditional approach to shearing.

"There's an advantage to the farmer, because it leaves a little bit more wool on the sheep. For years, in New Zealand, the principal reason they were still blade shearing there is it protects the sheep from sudden changes in weather."

Without the buzz from electric shears and having to keep the sheep oriented to the power source, Ford feels more relaxed with his blades, which he spends a couple of hours out of the box adjusting with tape to control how they close and fit in his hand, a strap keeping it all in place. "The shearer always transmits that lack of tension to the sheep."

He's quick to add, "Very good machine shearers like Gwen are also at ease, but a lot of beginners think it's going to be easier with a machine, and it isn't. Overall, according to professional shearers in New Zealand who do it both ways, it's physically easier to shear by hand. You don't do as many, but you don't have to control the sheep quite as rigidly. The powered hand piece will drive the shearer because it's always going. It wants to be in the wool."

Ford carries a handmade wooden toolbox with him, complete with shoulder carrying strap, hanging pocket watch, lubricating oils, a hardwood stick with a notch in it for blade sharpening, and a mechanical counter to keep track of how many he's sheared each day, since he gets paid per animal.

He also keeps a pail of water handy to wash off the lanolin that accumulates on his shears.

"These sheep are not very greasy, but there's some degree of lanolin in most sheep."

That grease can bulk up the best of shears and make them sticky, but these Leyden sheep, raised for meat that's sold to Hope & Olive and Green Fields Market in Greenfield, and at farmers markets in Amherst and Northampton, are out enough to get rained on, so much of their lanolin has washed out.

Each pair of shears is good for shearing about a thousand sheep. He figures he shears about four thousand sheep a year, about four times more than the Wisconsin woman he thinks of as his only possible counterpart in this country.

Dressed in a sleeveless black T-shirt from the 2008 Golden Shears World Shearing & Woolhandling Championships in Bjerken, Norway, Ford says he's been to plenty of competitions.

"There are farmers and judges from all over the place who judge you while you're shearing, and they judge the sheep for any nicks or ridges of wool left on and tags ... and, of course, time. But the quality is usually decisive."

He laughs modestly when asked if he's ever won.

With no shortage of top-notch contestants from countries that have lots more shearers, plenty more sheep and way more blade shearing than we have in this country, he says, "It would be pretty outrageous if I won. There's just a culture of sport shearing in places like Australia and New Zealand." And South Africa has won a good share of top titles in recent years. "They shear ten million sheep a year over there, and most shearing there is done with blades."

Although some say that the relentless wrestling, restraining, and releasing of sheep all day long is like running a marathon, Ford says, "It's just something you develop stamina for."

Since most sheep farms shear their flocks once a year, he keeps busy from February until at least August and often into the fall. Some breeds, like Icelandic sheep or angora goats, are shorn twice a year, and between Ford's own migration to shear in the South and his hand-cutting of firewood in winter, he says, "I stay in shape. I get out and it keeps me limber."

Most of the flocks he shears are small, and his limit for going it alone with his shears is about forty sheep, like at Northfield's Balky Farm. With larger herds—up to the four hundred or so sheep he does in Great Barrington each fall—he asks for a second shearer or maybe a third.

🏵 🏵 🏵

In the barn with a sheep's white head secured between his legs, Ford and the sheep are mellow as he softly snips off the wool from around the hip bone, bunching the wool up in with one hand to get as much as he can with a single clip.

As he constantly maneuvers his hand with an understanding of the sheep and its body, he's at ease in talking with Duprey. Clip, clip, clip go the pointy blades, which he deftly moves around the ewe's udder.

"It's not a finger thing. It's a forearm motion, and the position of the hand is constantly varying too, so it's not a constant tension," he says, where muscle fatigue or carpal tunnel injuries can set in.

While shearing, Ford calls the farmer over because he finds a redness on one animal, a sore on another. The farmer then marks the sheep with orange or red dye and makes a mental note to follow up with special attention.

"It's the only time you can see the bodies on them," Duprey says, taking advantage of the opportunity for close inspection.

Aside from the obvious reason that it keeps his flock comfortable in warmer weather, Duprey says annual shearing is important so his animals aren't dragging around an ever growing, unmanageable mess. It's certainly not because the wool is very valuable, he adds.

Last year, the market for wool was so poor that he dumped it. There are few places to process wool, and by the time he and Nicholas pay to have it transported, it pays for little more than the shearing.

"If we didn't shear, I think they'd probably die at some point, whether from heat exhaustion or some complication from excess weight, because they lie down and can't get back up," says Duprey.

Last year, an Australian ram shorn for the first time yielded eighty-nine pounds of wool, enough for thirty sweaters and nearly half its body weight.

There are a couple of sheep that manage to elude shearing each year, but the real danger is that, if they lie down on manure and then attract flies, maggots can get into the wool and actually begin feeding on the sheep.

As for Ford, shearing by hand is way more than a chore. There's fulfillment in fleecing.

"There's an athleticism to it," he says. And although the thought of sheep after sheep may be enough for the weary among us to doze off, "Every sheep is different. Every situation is different. Your skills always are being challenged, and you're always attempting to do the best job you can."

Randy Kehler delivers a speech at War Resisters' League conference, Haverford, Pennsylvania, on August 28, 1969.

photo by Theodore Brinton Hetzel by permission from
Daniel Ellsburg Papers Collection, Special Collections and
University Archives, University of Massachusetts, Amherst, Libraries

Driven by Conscience

January 20, 2018

Randy Kehler, whom I met when he was a candidate in a county commissioner's race soon after I'd arrived as a reporter, remained a conspicuously committed character around the region and beyond. His actions—for peace, campaign finance reform, nuclear disarmament and more— were covered by me as well as my newspaper colleagues and journalists around the nation.

This story combines reporting from January 20, 2018 and April 11, 1997, along with a series of interviews in 2021, after I had retired from the Recorder.

❂ ❂ ❂

Mention Randy Kehler's name to many people around western Massachusetts, and he'll be remembered as the tax resister who had his house seized by the IRS for non-payment of taxes.

But Kehler, who along with his wife, Betsy Corner, had their Colrain home taken for refusing for a dozen years to pay what they called "war taxes," continues to live a life defined by opposition to war and violence.

Now in his late seventies, on a hot July day in 2022 in his Shelburne Falls living room, the graying political activist looks back on that battle as well as imprisonment for refusing the Vietnam War draft, leadership of a national weapons freeze campaign, and inspiration for Daniel Ellsberg's release of the Pentagon Papers.

photo by Paul Franz

Randy Kehler, pacifist

The soft-spoken pacifist says that a life of acting out his conscience "obviously gave me a sense of personal satisfaction. It made me feel good about my life and who I was and what I was trying to do, even though I met with so little success."

The measure of success, though, can be elusive.

Federal agents came knocking at the door of the two-bedroom Shelburne Line Road house in Colrain in early March 1989 to hand deliver a notice for G. Randall Kehler and Corner saying the IRS was seizing it for $26,917.11 in back taxes owed since 1977.

The couple, strong opponents of the Vietnam War, were part of the Pioneer Valley War Tax Resisters League. Its members refused to pay taxes used for war, and the couple had seen their $743 bank account seized a couple of years earlier.

The three-year saga brought hundreds of protesters to the Valley Community Land Trust property for round-the-clock vigil for more than a year and a half, drawing national attention. The home was eventually sold at auction to a young couple, and Kehler, his wife and dozens of others were arrested for refusing to vacate the premises.

The vigil ended in May 1993 when Franklin County Superior Court issued an injunction to remove protesters from the land.

One of the lasting outcomes of the groundswell of support for the couple's action was creation of Building Our Swords into Plowshares, a nonprofit, volunteer organization that constructed two homes in Greenfield for low-income people.

The ordeal, Kehler recalls, "was exhausting for us. It was a frustrating time for me, how the ripples went on in the community," along with the fact that "the story about the house and about two families fighting over the house" became the focus for many people rather than "money spent on the military instead of meeting human needs."

Yet, "I look back on this as an event that affected not just Betsy and me, our neighbors and supporters, but it was part of the history of the whole wider community. I have absolutely no regrets about our having done it."

🞚 🞚 🞚

Randy Kehler's lifetime of activism may have slowed dramatically in recent years as he's dealt more with declining health than international affairs, but his concern over matters of conscience did not wane and were strongly felt even as he was growing up in Scarsdale, New York, and then attending Exeter Academy and Harvard.

One of four children of a "nominally Republican, never really successful businessman" and his "nominally Democratic" wife who headed the local church education program and played piano, Kehler grew up playing trumpet and participating in swimming, soccer, lacrosse, and football in high school but was not politically active.

At Exeter, where he completed his last two high school years, Kehler remembers defending a roommate bullied for being Jewish— and tearing his knee in the fight that ensued.

In 1965, between sophomore and junior years at Harvard, where he majored in government, Kehler taught at a Rwandan refugee camp in Tanganyika. The Vietnam War had been ramping up along with opposition to it on campus.

He was not yet tuned into antiwar fervor. But before leaving for the student-run program, a friend who'd also taken part in the African project told him, "Wait 'til you come back and you've experienced a year or more living in a Third World country. You'll be against the war then."

Kehler returned from teaching Tutsi refugees from Rwandan genocide, and his life indeed had changed. Over the last two summers and during his last year at Harvard, he moved to Roxbury, where he volunteered in youth summer and after-school programs.

"All of the families on my block were Black. That was where my focus was. I just sort of hung in there with my courses at Harvard the best I could. I wasn't a great or particularly serious student," yet Kehler did graduate in 1967 cum laude.

His time in Africa had changed him.

"I could imagine something kids with my background would have no way of imagining—what life was like in places where people were hungry, in refugee camps, going through horrible wars. That turned me against the war, and I did one thing after another that got me deeper and deeper in trouble with the draft. That's what turned my life around."

After returning from Tanganyika, Kehler worked against the war, encouraging fellow students to write letters to Congress. He, along with other Harvard students, signed a "Hell, no, we won't go" pledge to break the law rather than fight in Vietnam—a pledge that became a full-page ad in the *Harvard Crimson*.

After Harvard, he decided to study education at Stanford, where he was offered a fellowship.

"I had totally had it with Harvard, with the East Coast, the Boston area. The stuffiness of it, the conservativeness of it. I just wanted to get out to California, where everything was happening. I went out there, and within a couple of weeks I met some draft resisters, I tore up my draft card, I put it in the mail, I sent it back. That was September 1967. As soon as I did that, I felt I had crossed the Rubicon."

Kehler lasted for three weeks at Stanford's college of education before getting arrested in an October 1967 civil disobedience action, then turned his attention to the "free university" where he signed up for a course in Gandhian nonviolence through which he met Joan Baez and joined the War Resisters League.

"I was so impressed by their spirit of discipline and camaraderie, and their willingness to get arrested. When they sat down in the street to block buses, I found myself leaping into line and sitting down with them," recalls Kehler, whose first ten-day sentence at the Santa Rita County Jail followed by a forty-five-day sentence for a subsequent arrest "opened up a whole new thing in my mind: I soon realized there were more than a few older men and women. One was a dentist, one was a professional landscaper, one was an executive for Sierra Club. They all had families. I understood students and young people doing this, but what are *they* doing here? They'd been doing stuff like that periodically all their lives because that's who they were: ardent pacifists who also led very ordinary middle-class and professional lives."

They became role models for Kehler. He returned his draft card to the Selective Service as an act of protest, went to a sit-in at the Oakland

Induction Center and then a demonstration at the San Francisco Federal Building, where he was approached by two men in suits.

"They said, 'Excuse me, are you Randy Kehler? We'd like to interview you for a few minutes. Would you mind coming around the corner with us?'

"I said, 'That would be fine.' I thought they were from the media. They took me out from the sight of the crowd, grabbed me, and said, 'You're under arrest, for violation of the draft law.'"

The FBI agents, he recalls, "were picking off organizers, people whose names like mine were in the newspapers."

The arrest didn't stop Kehler from antiwar organizing activities, at least until February 1970, when he went on trial in Cheyenne, Wyoming. It was in Wyoming that Kehler had first registered for the draft in 1962, when he'd turned eighteen during a pre-college summer ranch job haying.

So Kehler, who was twenty-five at the time of his FBI arrest and had recently been indicted for refusing to cooperate with the Selective Service, was a speaker at an August 1969 War Resisters International conference in Haverford, Pennsylvania, showcasing young men already either in prison for opposing the war or—like himself—about to face trial.

❁ ❁ ❁

It was there that Ellsberg, a former Pentagon analyst, had been sitting in the back of the room, listening to the young speaker talk about imprisoned antiwar protesters.

Ellsberg, Kehler recalls, "was still trying to figure out where he was with the war, given that he was convinced that it was wrong, horribly brutal, and taking so many lives. What could he do about it?"

"He was shy and kind of reluctant" at the conference, where other participants included German pastor Martin "first they came for the Jews . . . " Niemöller, recalls Kehler. "Ellsberg knew he would be a fish out of water. He was on the fence about what he could do but was not so much on the fence about the war being absolutely wrong and that it needed to stop."

Kehler "opened my eyes to the possibilities of resisting the war," Ellsberg would write later ... "No Randy Kehler, no Pentagon Papers."

In the 2020 documentary film, *The Boys Who Said No,* a tearful Ellsberg tells Kehler, "When I heard you say these words, 'I'm going to prison,' it's as if an ax had split my head. But what had really happened was that my life had split in two. And it's my life after I heard those words that I've lived ever since."

The *New York Times* began publishing the Pentagon Papers on June 13, 1971, and by the time the *Washington Post* followed suit five days later after the Nixon administration halted their *Times* publication, Kehler had begun reading the *Times* accounts in his federal prison cell at La Tuna Penitentiary in west Texas, thanks to a gift subscription from Ellsberg.

There, Kehler was serving sixteen months of his twenty-four-month sentence for resisting military service, and he read each day's front-page story based on the leaked top secret defense department study.

Although the Pentagon Papers, which also were published in more than a dozen other newspapers, may not have been thoroughly read by all that many people, they helped end the war because of the response by Nixon to stop their publication and going after Ellsberg, Kehler says.

"The *New York Times* had every day a new across-the-front-page headline about something else revealed in the papers. And the *Post* did the same. People could see without reading the papers themselves," that for years presidents and the Pentagon had been lying about the war, which resulted in the deaths of roughly sixty thousand US troops and millions of Vietnamese military and civilian deaths as well as others around the region by the time the war ended in 1975.

Years later, Ellsberg recounted that after a tearful Kehler had told the Haverford gathering about going to prison for what he believed would be the right thing, "I left the auditorium and found a deserted men's room. I sat on the floor and cried for over an hour, just sobbing. The only time in my life I've reacted to something like that. Randy Kehler never thought his going to prison would end the war. If I hadn't met Randy Kehler, it wouldn't have occurred to me to copy the documents. His actions spoke to me as no mere words would have done. He put the right question in my mind at the right time."

Kehler says of the Pentagon Papers, "To me, it underlies the whole question of government secrecy. It totally undermines democracy. People can't make informed decisions when they don't know what the hell's going on. They're being told lies."

Months after the Haverford conference, at the 1970 federal trial, Kehler's parents testified, they were "very upset" that he'd violated the draft law and faced prison. Yet he recalls his father telling the judge, "Your honor, if you want to put somebody in prison, you should put me in, because my son's values are what we taught him. So it's our fault."

"I cry every time I think of that," says Kehler. "I never, ever thought he would say that. Because he was just a retired businessman, a Republican with suit and tie, and very conservative, I probably got only a two-year sentence instead of three, four, or five years. Some part of him certainly identified with my position and my values."

Kehler served six months in a minimum-security prison in southern Arizona and sixteen months in Texas. He recalls playing washtub bass in a band with the mostly Latino inmates and also being dismissed from a prison job as a GED teacher after asking for copies of Hermann Hesse's *Siddhartha* for his students.

"I learned more in two years in prison than I ever learned in four years at Harvard. Prison was like a microcosm in some ways of the whole society. It was stratified in terms of education, wealth, connections, and privileges.

Following his release in 1972, Kehler and a friend traveled to Mexico to write about his experience. While in a Mexico City restaurant, they overheard English speakers who'd been teaching at the alternative Woolman Hill School in Deerfield, Massachusetts.

"I didn't know what I wanted to do. I thought that sounded interesting, so I joined up with them. In theory, I taught carpentry on the basis of six months in the prison carpentry shop. I knew almost nothing."

In a visit to New Mexico, he met Wally and Juanita Nelson, a tax resisting pacifist couple he'd read about, and convinced them in 1974 also to move to Woolman Hill to farm.

Kehler also taught Spanish at the school, where he met his wife, Betsy, employed there as an organic gardener.

After leaving the school in 1974, Kehler ran an unsuccessful campaign for county commissioner in 1976, bicycling to campaign events around the county because he didn't own a car, he remembers.

He followed that by becoming involved with the newly formed Traprock Peace Center. He launched a 1980 ballot referendum proposal calling for a nuclear weapons freeze that was approved in 59 of 62 Western Massachusetts cities and towns. That grew into creation of the National Nuclear Weapons Freeze Campaign to halt all testing, production, and deployment of nuclear weapons. It hired Kehler as national coordinator working out of a St. Louis, Missouri, headquarters. A freeze campaign resolution passed by the end of 1983 in 88 percent of 180 Vermont towns as well as 370 US city councils, 71 county councils, and nearly half the nation's state legislatures.

Kehler and Corner, who'd recently given birth to a daughter and helped create the Franklin County Land Trust, found living in a new place difficult during 1981 and 1982 and asked to move back to Franklin County. Eventually, he left the freeze campaign post, and the couple returned to the house that would be taken from them a few years later.

🞕 🞕 🞕

The prolonged house protest, which also landed Kehler and his wife in jail for refusing to leave the premises after the IRS auctioned it to another couple, became a national news story with Kehler and Corner featured on television on the *Phil Donahue Show*—the kind of reductionist spectacle that he recalls had audience members booing and heckling them as "draft dodgers" and "tax cheats." They paid local and state taxes and contributed the equivalent of their federal tax payments to local charities, says Kehler, but that seemed ignored.

He also worked on campaign finance reform efforts in Massachusetts and nationally from 1987 to 2001 and was among nine members of "the Democracy Brigade arrested in the US Capitol in 1999 protesting the Senate's refusal to take up legislation limiting "soft money contributions" while unfurling a thirty-foot banner: "Stop Crimes Against Democracy: End Finance Corruption Now."

The aftermath of the Colrain house ordeal, which left the couple feeling that some area residents hated them and even in one case resulted in him nearly being run over by a neighbor, Kehler claims, had them drained physically and emotionally.

"I felt like I was just wiped out," recalls Kehler, his voice shaking as he recounts details of the episode in their Shelburne Falls home where the couple moved in 2020.

He was soon diagnosed with chronic fatigue syndrome and remembers walking with a friend and "ending up in tears saying, 'I don't know how much longer I can take this. The pressure's too much.'

"A lot of it was just keeping it going, being the person on the spot day in and day out for all these supporters, bless their hearts, who were coming from all parts of everywhere to take their week in the vigil, to make sure they had what they needed, and that they were properly thanked, and then the constant press pressure and all the people hating us. This was not an event for a thin-skinned person, and I'm very thin-skinned."

Kehler's days now include reading books by his neighbor, poet Martin Estrada, Thich Nat Hanh, Abraham Joshua Heschel, and others. It's a quiet life spent meditating and playing meditative piano selections like Bach/Gounod's "Ave Maria" and staying connected with his daughter, two grandchildren, and friends, including Ellsberg.

In his late seventies, he retains the handsome, neat appearance that harkens back to his youthful draft-resister days as he looks back on a lifetime of taking action for his convictions.

Kehler recalls his mother asking him, "Why do you always try to take on a Don Quixote project? First you try to do total nuclear disarmament, then you try to take private money out of politics."

And then then he laughs softly at the recollection.

"What's motivated me to work on different political projects has never been any kind of realistic prospect of major change," he says. "I would have never done anything if I wanted for that to occur. In my lifetime, I can't think, on these issues I've worked on, that there's still been no indication of major change. But I do it because it goes to the heart of what's wrong. It gives me personal satisfaction not to be fussing around the edges of the problem, minimalist approaches that don't go to the heart of it. And I believe, perhaps wrongly, that's what most people want. Without any prospect of necessarily success, I just was motivated by working on what seemed to be getting to root of the problem."

A pause, and then he adds, "I'd like to be remembered as an optimist *doer* who like Don Quixote wasn't afraid to charge the windmill and could imagine the windmill coming down."

Kehler points back to a turning point as a nineteen-year-old student on a Congress of Racial Equality bus from Harlem to the 1963 March on Washington.

"I got on the bus at midnight, one of the last people to get on. There was only one seat available next to the only other white guy on the bus. No sooner did I get on the bus, he flips on an overhead light, hands me this open book, and says, 'Here. Read this.'"

It was the annual peace calendar of the War Resisters League, an organization Kehler had never heard of. It featured a war resister's story opposite each page. The profile his seatmate pointed to was of Max Sandin, who'd left his native Russia in 1910 rather than join the Czar's army and after immigrating refused to join the US Army in World War I or be drafted in World War II. Sandin then refused to pay "war" taxes for decades.

"I'd never heard of non-violence in my household, at school, at church, anywhere. Or about tax resistance to not pay for war," remembers Kehler, who soon realized that the man beside him was Sandin. "It was a huge turning point for me."

When they arrived in the nation's capital, he allowed Sandin, who used a cane, to take his arm as they walked together.

Kehler isn't blind to privilege in his life: growing up as a white man with money and what it could buy, the privilege of being in the right place at the right time, sitting by chance next to someone "who opened my eyes to nonviolence," or inspiring Daniel Ellsberg to take the action he did. And then there's the privilege, he says, of "being able to make something of it, by understanding the situation and being present. I'm very lucky."

Whenever he's given the privilege of speaking to young people, Kehler says, his voice cracking, "I tell them don't ever, ever, ever assume anything you do, particularly if it's an act of conscience, won't make a difference."

photo by Richie Davis
Hands of Time

Time for a Change in This Town

April 24, 1982

Whenever the day came to switch clocks to or from daylight-savings time, typically Recorder *photographer Chuck Blake, with his old-school humor, concocted an oddball visual reminder like an image of a sundial or a town clock being manipulated. In what was extremely atypical for a local newspaper, I dreamed up this fanciful story after wondering what happens where time zones meet. It took only a few minutes with a newsroom atlas to find the town of my dreams, in Indiana, and to begin making a series of phone calls.*

There's standard time, and there's daylight savings time.

Here in Ora, Indiana, you can have it both ways.

This unincorporated town on state Route 35, with a population of maybe 180, is partly in Starke County and partly in Pulaski (that "ski" is pronounced "sky") in northwestern Indiana.

The most confusing aspect of the town—although folks in Ora may not all agree on that either—is that it's in two different time zones.

Come Sunday at 2 a.m., Ora—in fact all of Indiana—will come together for the first time since last October 25. Then next October, when millions of people across America turn their clocks back, it will again become a tale of two time zones in Ora.

In all, seventeen of Indiana's ninety-two counties align themselves with Central Standard Time: primarily those in the extreme northwest within metropolitan Chicago and the extreme southwest around Evansville.

Sunday, they turn their clocks an hour ahead to Central Daylight Time, joining the rest of the state, which remains in Eastern Standard Time year-round.

Fall and winter, most of Indiana—and half of Ora—aligns itself with its neighbors to the east. Spring and summer, all of Indiana unites, synchronizing with abutters to the west.

"When I was a kid growing up in the fifties, it was really confusing," admits Jean Weimer, director of the Indiana division of the state library in Indianapolis. "One year, they'd change to daylight time and summer. How often I wished they would. The next year they wouldn't. There were fights between the state legislature and the federal government. For a few years, we were switching time zones every summer. How I wished they would put Indiana in one zone or the other completely. We're just sort of caught."

But compared to Ora, Ms. Weimer has it easy. She's in the state capital, about a hundred miles southeast of the little town time forgot.

After all, half of Ora is in one of those seventeen Indiana counties that swing west on "slow" (Central) time. The Pulaski County half of town swings with the rest of the state and "fast" (Eastern) time.

Because it's unincorporated, there's no town hall or town clock to deal with in Ora.

The Tippecanoe River slices through the municipality but doesn't establish county boundaries. It just rolls along, perhaps oblivious to the town that doesn't even plan to observe its own centennial in the summer . . . a town that residents say lost its zip after the pickle factory and other firms shut down.

"It is kind of teeny-weeny," said Richard Thompson, postmaster in the town of Monterey, five miles from Ora in Pulaski County. Some of his motor route patrons are in Ora.

"It's only four or five miles west of me and it's only one o'clock over there when it's two o'clock here. You just remember when you climb in your car that there's going to be an hour's difference."

To Kenneth Mahler, who cleans boilers and furnaces, "It's a very messed up affair in . . . a small, little, one-horse town."

"We keep our clocks to correspond to where we work. Most people know we've got two different time zones here." Without keeping two clocks side by side in their houses and without a pair of watches on their wrists, Ora folks keep punctual, either on "fast" time or on "slow" time.

"If you're supposed to meet someone, you just make sure you keep straight in your head to meet them "on their time, whichever time they may be on."

But imagine if you work up north, in Knox, and your spouse works down in Winamac. How do you keep your clocks then? Or maybe your kids go to school in Monterey, but you work in Plymouth? Then, said Donna Wallers, who with her husband runs Wallers's (grocery) Store, the situation does become messy.

"They're going in every which direction," she says. "Someday, we'll all be back on the same time."

But if some people here mark their time "fast," and others mark it "slow," Richard Thompson is unfazed by it all.

"Some of 'em are . . ., some of 'em aren't," says Thompson, whose bait shop he claims to be "the best one in northern Indiana." Whether it's Central, Daylight Savings, Eastern, Mountain, Pacific, or whatever, "It don't make no difference to us," Thompson says.

"We're all low-geared here. We don't care about clocks."

Jennifer Rosner and Bill Corwin enjoy time with their daughters, Sophia Corwin, left, and Juliet Corwin.

A Silent World

August 7, 2010

The book about parenting two deaf sisters caught my eye when it appeared in the newsroom, and meeting with its author helped me discover intricacies of a deaf culture that I found remarkable.

⊠ ⊠ ⊠

Jennifer Rosner had just completed her doctorate in philosophy from Stanford University when she gave birth to her first child.

But no academic degree could brace her for the shock of discovering, in the first hours of her infant daughter's life, that newborn Sophia had failed a hearing test.

The thirty-four-year-old woman and her husband—a children's advocacy lawyer—wrestled for months with the possibility, the likelihood, the reality that their infant was severely deaf.

"For months, I'd go in and out of grief moments balanced by the joy of this incredible, tiny, beautiful, little baby. It was a very mixed up, emotional time," recalls Rosner. "We didn't understand deafness, what her future would be. We were scared. We didn't know what limitations she would have, and they were all scary."

Her recent memoir of her struggle to share her love of the aural world with her two daughters, *If a Tree Falls* from Feminist Press, describes an odyssey that drew her through her relationship with her own mother, through past generations of deafness, and through controversial issues within the deaf community.

"A family's quest to hear and be heard" is the subtitle of the Leverett author's first book.

Rosner and her husband, Bill, were so committed to ensuring Sophia's future that, after researching schools, they relocated from California to western Massachusetts so she could attend Clarke Schools for Hearing and Speech in Northampton.

"I think when you have a baby with a special issue, you're looking at it as a focus, and you're not really looking at a whole child as much as you ought to be," says Rosner. "Then, you finally have the perspective to see how this is a child who's going to flourish."

But along the way, the path was anything but clear.

First of all, giving birth to a deaf child raised for Rosner the issue of her relationship with her own mother, whose deafness caused a distance between the two when she was growing up.

"I couldn't fix her attention on my being," Rosner's book says. "My chatter, my questions, even my songs—nothing could retrieve her. She was distracted, lost in her own thoughts. I called out for her, still waiting. Couldn't my mother hear me?"

Her mother, who had a hearing loss caused by severe childhood infections, had four children to raise. Rosner now understands that it was probably "easy to just retreat from all the input. You can just tune it all out, take out your hearing aid, and you know where to go that hearing people don't, to regroup, to recharge. There's a positive aspect to that, too."

As she returned home from the hospital with her newborn daughter, Rosner received a fax from her father. It was a family tree with asterisks beside six names indicating "deaf and dumb." There were two sisters—her great-aunts—along with three of their children and also a cousin, all of whom were deaf.

That sent Rosner—who'd never been told her family members had hearing problems—back through census and other records trying to uncover whether her daughter's deafness was hereditary.

A geneticist had assured her parents when they were about to have children that there was no hereditary pattern of deafness, and Rosner and her husband were offered the same assurance by another geneticist after Sophie's birth.

"Everyone wanted to explain away deafness with other causes," Rosner says. But after the birth six years ago of their second daughter Juliet, who was even more profoundly deaf, it became clear that the young couple were both carrying recessive genes for deafness.

In her journal and in her book, Rosner writes a fictionalized account of what the experience of deafness must have been like 125 years ago before technology was available to detect deafness and foster hearing and before the shifting of attitudes that had historically labeled the non-speaking deaf as lacking understanding.

"I needed these ancestors," her memoir says. "I needed them for guidance. I needed them for company. I needed them for escape."

Rosner also needed a closeness with her baby to deal with her anxieties.

"I just wanted to hold her all the time. It was worry that caused extra engagement. That was one of the luckiest things we had: that it didn't interfere with our bond."

Compelled to heighten contact through touch, Rosner feels lucky that the response by her husband and her to their daughter was to stay connected by consciously being expressive in other ways.

"It meant not taking anything for granted, like I can talk to you while I'm putting these things on the shelf and not paying any attention. I'm forced do all these tactile things and have more skin-to-skin interaction."

As a mother wondering whether her daughter's future world be closed off to many of the simple enjoyments we take for granted, she contemplated getting Sophia hearing aids, having the family learn sign language, and teaching her to speak. That's when Rosner encountered a sometimes militant split within the deaf community between an oral approach favoring hearing aids and learning speech and a signing contingent that encourages a distinctly deaf culture that doesn't bow to standards of a hearing world.

"Everywhere we went, my own ears burned with what she missed—a snippet of Mozart through a neighbor's window, the tap-tap of a woodpecker on the forest path, the soft trickle of water at the stream. On our walks, I shifted Sophia from the stroller to the baby carrier so that she could feel the vibrations of my voice. Then I'd force myself to speak about the scene around us.

"'See that bird? That's a robin. Robins eat worms. And they sing, Sophia. They sing beautiful bird songs.'"

Rosner not only worried about whether her daughter would ever be able to share in a whisper or have a phone conversation. She feared, too, that she would not be able to share an intimate connection with her daughter.

"All you want is for your child to have every possible opportunity to have a healthy, happy life. It took a while to understand that deafness wasn't going to impinge on her wellness."

But she adds, "For me, it's hard to imagine what a life without sound could be like. I love music, I love nature. I go on a walk, and the trickle of a stream is very subtle, but it means so much to me. To miss those things that enrich your life was heartbreaking, from the perspective of a listener, to think that that would be missing."

Even though she tried to imagine "beauties that come with the silence," Rosner had her three-month-old daughter fitted with hearing devices and took every opportunity to help her notice sounds and learn speech, as well as sign.

By the time the family moved to Northampton, where Sophia was immediately enrolled in Clarke's parent-infant program, they were assured by program director Janice Gatty that their nine-month-old daughter was alert, engaged, and connected with a family that was intact.

☒ ☒ ☒

When she gave birth to her second daughter, Juliet, Rosner's fears resurfaced. Juliet, she learned, was profoundly deaf. In fact, those fears intensified because for weeks the infant arched her back and refused to make eye contact. Could it be Usher syndrome? Could her daughter be blind as well?

Juliet, she now believes, was simply trying to make sense of her environment, to "get visual information from all over."

A matter of weeks after her birth, Juliet was enrolled in Clarke School's parent-infant program. Soon the family was being tutored at home in sign language. And at age one, Juliet had cochlear implant surgery to provide direct electrical stimulation to the auditory nerve.

"We really worked on sign before the implant," Rosner says. "That year, I was worried she would not have any language. With Sophia, I was scared that if she signed, it would be harder for her to speak. It's all false, but at the time, that's how I felt.

"We have to pick a track," she continues. "That's how fractious the worlds are. Everyone feels you have to be either this or that. When you don't know what you're doing and you're afraid and people are giving you arguments about how one will impact the other, it's confusing."

Both daughters are now mainstreamed at Leverett Elementary School. With a pair of the girls' Suzuki violin cases resting on a table and their self-portraits hanging from the refrigerator, Rosner and her family have settled into life as a family like any other.

"Now, we have the luxury where we're very much up and running in an auditory world with them," says Rosner, though she recalls taking special precautions like having to chase Juliet running toward the ocean at the beach—where both daughters have to remove their hearing devices—because the young girl can't hear her mother's warnings about the strong undertow.

There are still special considerations like reminding friends at a sleepover that once the lights and hearing devices are turned off, her daughters won't hear anything said in the darkness. Or that they won't hear anything said in a whisper or hurriedly unless there's deliberate effort to connect.

As the parent of deaf children, Rosner has also had to make sure that teachers and friends are aware of situations when additional cues are needed to compensate for ones the hearing world takes for granted.

"While they're auditory, they always need visual reinforcement," Rosner says. "When a teacher writes on the board, talks, and turns around, that will all get lost. There are ways in which the technology is definitely great, but that doesn't completely make you hearing. There will be idioms and other things that are completely lost. You have to watch for odd gaps you wouldn't expect."

There are also plenty of joys for Rosner, like watching the special relationship that's developed between her mother and her daughters, who share a common bond in deafness and in living with hearing devices.

Like her mother, Rosner says, her daughters occasionally remove their hearing devices to take a temporary, meditative break from the auditory world's stimulation and the effort it demands.

It's restorative also for Rosner—a verbal person formally trained in "sense of self-concept in relation to disability"—to overcome her fears that she and her husband wouldn't be able to express complex feelings with their children.

Throughout her book, Rosner uses the metaphor of a string tied between the wrists of her ancestors and their deaf children to show how they stayed connected despite the limitations of language.

If a Tree Falls expresses an essential longing to connect, yet Rosner is becoming more confident about how her daughters' lives are unfolding.

"Watching my girls grow was a most restorative experience for me."

Juliet wrote a small book, *Animals*, with help from a teacher, that ends with an autobiographical note:

> The author is deaf, so when she takes out her cochlear implants, she can't hear you. But she can hear a little. She understands sign language and can read your lips. She plays violin and loves singing, reading and writing. She was six when she wrote and drew this.

photo by Suzanne Webber

Al Miller, Vietnam War veteran

Healing the Deep Wounds of War

November 12, 2002

I can't recall how I heard about Al Miller's volunteer work with the Veterans Education Project, an organization that sends veterans into Western Massachusetts high schools to discuss the harsh realities of war. But Miller, a writer, farmer and carpenter, made a visceral impression that's lasted for decades by honestly sharing his powerful story with me, just as he has with others who have met him.

✾ ✾ ✾

Al Miller looks out on a sea of young faces in the high school classroom he's visiting, and he struggles to relate his experience.

"I can remember being in American history class when I was sixteen or seventeen, and I wasn't concerned with lessons of American history," he says, trying to reach across the divide. "I didn't think it was anything that would touch my life."

All in the space of a profound minute:

A "boy" of nineteen or twenty is asleep in a hammock when Miller—then just a year or two older—enters the Vietnamese hooch, or hut, and awakens him, ordering him outside. Then, in a split-second judgment fueled by fear that the sleepy young man has a gun he's going to pull, Miller shoots first with his automatic rifle.

"I looked down," recalls Miller, gazing off into the distance. "It's not an event that occurs like Hollywood. People don't die immediately. He was wanting to hold onto life. I could numb out, but I stayed with it. It bridged something."

At first, Miller wants to take back his act. He wishes it were a dream, averts his eyes from his struggling victim, then tries labeling him "gook" as if to rationalize the killing. Then he has the immediate sense that those enemy labels no longer hold together to disconnect him nor to overwhelm the humanity of the person he's murdering.

He tries rationalizing by dredging up from his gut the image of another young soldier in his company who was blown up on patrol a week or so earlier. "Daniel, this one's for you," he tells himself, trying to clear his own guilt for failing to warn his buddy of the danger.

In the same instant, Miller remembers his uncle back in Missouri who'd always railed against him and his brothers any time they caused another creature to suffer. And so Miller shoots his Vietnamese victim again to end his suffering.

Afterward, his platoon enters the hut and returns with photos from the dead man's wallet, images from a human life: the kid with his worried-looking mother, another with his siblings, another with his extended family. The pain, the remorse, reverberates out of the destroyed human before him "like a logarithmic spiral."

Miller's eyes fill with tears as he revisits those few, precious moments. They have weighed heavily on his psyche for decades in recurring dreams from which he awakened night after night in a cold sweat, clutching his sheet and feeling "the deficit in my soul for having taken a human life."

The last time he was haunted—four nights in a row—by a dream of being chased through the woods, Miller whispered to himself in the moments before wakefulness, "I am a murderer."

The spell was broken.

By connecting with his Vietnamese victim in those moments in the hut, Miller recalls, "I felt like l was with him in his passing. What he wanted in life was to live in community and respect. I told myself, 'I'll find higher values in myself.'"

Miller pauses to reflect. Then he adds, "I came to realize there may not be any higher values than to live in community and respect."

❊ ❊ ❊

At fifty-four, William Allen Miller is a tall man with long, wavy gray hair and a mellow voice that tells his story softly and slowly. When he moved to the area from Colorado in 1983, it was to learn furniture making at Leeds Design School in Easthampton. He read a news story about Buddhist monks building a peace pagoda in Leverett and was drawn to it.

"I wanted to come up, but I was afraid to, because of what I had experienced in Vietnam. Yet I was afraid to reveal what I had done."

When he finally found the courage to visit the pagoda, he recalls, "I felt an acceptance in a literal, visceral way that I had never felt before. It was that sense of, 'It doesn't matter what you bring.'"

At the pagoda, where he would come to live for fifteen months, the monks showed slides of their visit to Vietnam. They conveyed the nation's poverty borne of the US embargo after the war—and the war itself. Miller was so moved by what he saw that he had to make peace within himself as well as make a statement through fasting.

Kato-Shonin, the pagoda's head monk, convinced him to first make a pilgrimage to Vietnam, to give himself support for the fast. For three weeks in the summer of 1989, Miller visited hospitals from Hanoi to Saigon, toured orphanages around the country, and met with combatants.

"It was a very powerful trip," he recalls. "I encountered veterans who were there of their own volition, painting orphanages and doing clinics. It was really uplifting," particularly since no one sought notoriety for their actions—not the double-amputee from Wisconsin taking medical aid into the country, not the American woman helping to find adoptive homes for Amer-Asian children in the orphanages.

Miller fasted for forty days, beginning on his birthday, until October 2. He spent four hours of each day on the steps of the US Capitol. The following year, he traveled to Vietnam with fellow veterans, meeting in Hanoi a Vietnamese ex-colonel who had taken part in the same military encounter when a round of ammunition bounced off his helmet and took out one side of his collar bone and his shoulder blade.

"We both stood up, walked around the table, and greeted and embraced each other," recalls Miller, seated in the kitchen of the Leverett pagoda's zendo.

He was attracted to the pagoda to help heal his 1969 and 1979 inner wounds from Vietnam and to commune with the spirit of the people he confronted there.

"Buddhism resonates with my experience as a way to live with respect and community. It resonates very deeply," says Miller. Yet at first he feared, "How do I go there and hold what I hold and face those people day after day?"

When he finally revealed his dark secret to Kato Shonin, the monk's compassion soothed him. "Your experience there is your prayer of the preciousness of life," Kato said.

It is Buddhist ritual, Miller believes, that has helped him reconnect with his sense of self after severing his own humanity through taking another person's life.

"I held myself back from the full benefits of community for the last thirty years except for being with a few very close people. I stayed on the periphery of society. We talk of healing a flesh wound— I expected that I'd someday heal the psyche like that. That still hasn't happened, but it's changed a lot. Ritual has done more to move my sense of being with my experiences than anything else I've ever encountered."

Two years ago, in a ceremony of offerings, Miller rededicated himself for the shooting of three young Vietnamese he stumbled upon one day. They had weapons slung over their shoulders. He shot them.

Now, he says, "I'm trying to become a human being."

❀ ❀ ❀

Going into Hanoi the first time on his first post-war visit, Miller watched an old man herd hundreds of ducks toward a rice paddy covered with lotus blossoms across a road where bicycles, water buffalos, and foot traffic marked the pace of humanity.

"I asked myself 'What is here that is my enemy? What's the justification for attacking this?'" Miller asks, then answers his own question in a single word: "Insanity."

"What I had to embrace before I could fire bullets into a body was my own dehumanization," he says. "That's necessary for everyone before we can declare war, and we live in denial of that. I can't attack somebody outside myself and not injure myself."

As Miller, a member of the Veterans Education Project, goes into schools and speaks to young audiences who look to a future of war with Iraq, he struggles with conveying his own unfathomable experiences.

"How do you communicate your sense that war is the ultimate failure of every possibility of human creativity, intellect, compassion, grace, dignity? There's nothing sane in the choices you have to make in combat."

Miller, awarded a medal for bravery and valor, believes now that it would have felt more courageous to face the "cultural and familial shame of going to Canada. It was easier to kill than to say no."

Recalling the horrors, Miller says, "I wish that I could take everyone into the ward in Japan where I spent the night listening to teenagers crying, 'Nurse, nurse, my stumps are bleeding.' And to look into the eyes alone and see the old men in those bodies, to share the devastation of that."

Still, he feels that his message gets through, and that helps in his own renewal.

"I wish that someone had given me a different perspective than movies on the reality of violence. I get letters from students. I've never been able to read five of them at a time. Their expressions are overwhelming. At times it's a kind of salve for my wounds."

And he knows he's not alone.

"There's a huge community in the woods—and the woods of their minds—vets who experience the same thing," Miller says. "We're still hurting and still wondering how to tell other people."

Now that Miller has gone back and studied the history of Vietnam that he never knew as a young soldier, he's grown cynical of the political motivations, machinations, and consequences of labeling and then killing the so-called enemy in the name of justice.

"So we go off again half-cocked," he laments, "creating the next generation of victims of violence."

photo by Paul Franz

Tim de Christopher, sculptor

Emerging from Stone

May 13, 2006

*There's magic in bringing out a wild lightness from a huge
hunk of cold stone that drew me to write this and other features
I did about Tim de Christopher, whose ability to imagine an
entire world within the rock as he carves still fascinates me.*

❖ ❖ ❖

The man, bald and looking a lot like the late actor Peter Lorre, is
barely pint-sized— maybe four feet in height. And there's a deafening
buzzing that fills the former auto body shop you walk through to get
to him.

"I don't know his name. He hasn't fully introduced himself," says
Tim de Christopher once the din has ended from the pneumatic
hammer he's using to create a stone sculpture of a stocky Asian-looking
man clutching a dove to his chest with his left arm, a flower in his right
hand. "He's lovingly known in the community as Shorty."

Wearing a brown work shirt and gray work cap in the Third Street,
former Chick's Garage studio filled with odd, sculpted pieces and an
array of chisels, the fifty-one-year-old sculptor seems only slightly less
quirky than his white Indiana limestone creation. But then again,
Turners Falls is a quirky place, with a stone carver working on his
cathedral project inside what was originally a Pontiac dealership.

The studio will be open to the public as part of the upcoming Arts and Blooms downtown walking tour. The event will give people a chance to see de Christopher at work on pieces of cold stone packed with a little zaniness, human warmth, and wry humor.

There's *Adam and Eve,* for example, just back from a Stone Sculptors of New England show in Hardwick where they were in the center of a fifty-foot semicircle "serpent wall" of scale-like slate shingles. The premiere couple beneath a snake-bearing tree look off nervously with "uh-oh" eyes while out back, a bus—described by a shy but wickedly witty sculptor as "the 4:45 Greyhound out of Eden"—has a Ralph Kramden arm overhead: "Get out, Alice!"

A work in progress looks like a set of pipes or ducts—or is that one a duck coming out of an igloo?

"I'm not sure," says de Christopher, an unassuming napkin doodler who feigns the part of innocent bystander in his studio, waiting to see what will emerge as he carves away at stone. "I think it's one of my pipe machines, but it looked like a bird, so I gave it an eye."

The artist points at another work in progress with a tiny latter-day *Adam and Eve* peering out nervously from what could be a water tower or a citadel or the bottom of a stone seat.

"They're very curious guys," de Christopher says of the naked couple as he also looks out suspiciously from wide, round wire-rimmed glasses. "I don't know what's going on with them."

▩▩▩

And so the discovery process goes.

Sketches on napkins copied in pencil on stone reveal that there's some planning at work here, even if it changes in process. But de Christopher, who arrived in western Massachusetts in 1992 fresh from the stoneyard at St. John the Divine Cathedral in New York and then in Turners Falls about five years ago, insists there's a slow revelation as well, just as in life.

"Things move really slowly for the most part," he says. "It takes time for the evolutionary process."

Another one of those hard-to-define elements is health.

De Christopher was diagnosed with multiple sclerosis in 1987.

"It took me by surprise and for a whirl," said the stone carver, for whom the disease has been mostly dormant, yet sometimes acts up with numbness in his hands, feet, and legs and sometimes in dizziness or motor control problems.

"It's always an issue, but it's behaving itself," he says with a shrug and a nervous smile. "I don't pay much attention to it. I kind of like count my blessings. It's there, but it hasn't stopped me yet."

Though *Shorty* thought he was headed to a show this year at Forest Hill Cemetery outside Boston, de Christopher's application was rejected, "so he's just part of the gang." The artist shrugs it off as another case of "see what emerges."

Then there's Turners Falls, for instance, with its buzz about a blossoming River Culture arts community in what had been a nineteenth-century factory village that fell on hard times.

Turners, de Christopher's Cathedral Project, *Shorty*, and the rest—"like everything else, it's in this constantly evolving stage of wait and see."

❊ ❊ ❊

De Christopher, who grew up in the San Francisco Bay area and moved to New York to study design at Cooper Union in 1977, was steeped in art while still in the womb.

His father worked as a graphic designer, toy designer, product designer, and interior designer as well as host of his own TV drawing show for about ten years.

His grandfather, moreover, worked as a stone carver in Italian quarries from the age of nine before immigrating in his teens to this country about a century ago.

By the time de Christopher got to meet his grandfather, when he was about ten, the man had already retired.

"I never got to see him work," de Christopher says of the patriarch, who had worked his way up to carver in quarries around Naples. "He did the traditional stuff: Mary, Joseph, and Jesus. I grew up with all kinds of stories about my grandfather, the stone carver from Italy," who had started a monument business with his brother when he arrived in this country.

"As children, we'd play hide-and-seek and run around the tombstones in his front yard."

The young artist started in his father's footsteps when he headed off to study graphic design but soon found his way back to the path of his grandfather.

"I just had an urge to start carving," says de Christopher, who spent his sophomore year in Italy working beside the *artesiani* but doing his own sculpture.

"I was a foreigner, an artist, but I was working with the tradesmen. Some of their work was architecture. Some was purely sculpture.

After returning home to finish college, de Christopher worked for five years making architectural models before trying to earn an architecture degree.

But while studying at Columbia, the carving bug again got him—during a visit to the Cathedral of St. John the Divine, across and down the street a few blocks. Work on the cathedral, which had begun in 1892, stopped during World War II and hadn't resumed until 1979, with a stoneyard institute set up to train inner-city youths the trade of stone work.

"I'm there as a student with all the other architectural students," de Christopher recalls—"and there are my people carving stone!"

"I can do that," he mimes with a laugh.

A year and a half into his graduate studies, the ambivalent architect-in-training asked if there was need for another carver for the summer. He'd be the only Columbia student among African-American, Puerto Rican, German, Russian, Chinese, and French workers.

He was hired. He never returned to school.

"It made more sense to be there," recalls de Christopher, who carved for two years. The stoneyard, originally funded with an endowment, was now a commercial business, Cathedral Stoneworks, and was taking on private contracts.

Two gargoyles he carved there—a monkey and a devil—went not on a cathedral but on a new wing of the Jewish Museum on Fifth Avenue.

"They were having a labor dispute in the middle of the project. The monkey represented labor. The devil represented management. My boss suspected: 'Was that me?'"

▩ ▩ ▩

Stone's one of those heavy materials that can seem surprisingly light when sculpted with a sharp wit.

An elephant, for example, has a couple dancing on its back and someone riding behind its smiling head. And the elephant's on a little iron cart.

"That's my (first) wife's fiftieth anniversary present," de Christopher explains. "All the characters are people in our little world: her mother getting her hair done by one of our friends, who's a hairdresser. He's talking to another neighbor. That's another good friend who gives us a lot of help, driving us to the airport, as chauffeur. And there's me and Kathy, dancing our lives away." Another of their friends is in the rear, hanging out with the couple's dogs.

Many of the works, like *Shorty* or *Adam and Eve,* could someday be part of his *Cathedral Project,* an assemblage of sculptures that he imagines in the future as a large public collection unto itself.

De Christopher's Web site— www.timdechristopher.tumblr.com— described the *Cathedral Project* in 2001 as

> a monumental site-specific sculpture project to be built near the banks of the Connecticut River . . . telling an archetypal story of the human condition as it has manifested through time, in its own unique way, in the village of Turners Falls. From its difficult and tragic beginnings to its agricultural and industrial underpinnings, its present state, and uncertain future.

The artist first imagined his legacy project not that long following his arrival in the area in 1979 after two fellow workers from his New York crew had invited him for a weekend to their cabin in Heath. He was ready to leave New York anyway and moved the following year "from the Lower East Side to the heights of Shutesbury."

At the outset, he took on contract work from Cathedral Stoneworks, which closed in 1994, until his own sculpture and commissions took over.

One day, his partner at the time said, "Why don't you just build the damn cathedral? That's what you want to do!"

At first, de Christopher conceived of "a little building on a hill, an architectural space that had some sort of spiritual presence and essence to it."

As his idea grew more complex, more narrative, and larger in scale, the notion of a cathedral evolved. From a studio in the Greenfield Venture Center, he moved in 2001 to his own first Turners Falls studio, the former Williams Garage.

The giant, empty mill buildings began to evoke for him the same haunting spirituality.

"You walk into some of these large mill buildings, especially the abandoned mills, and they're just so huge. They just evoke a response in me," he says, going on to free-associate between church rituals and work rituals, church bells and work bells, "and you flow in to work and go to your posts in the factory, and you sharpen knives and weave linens and then the bell rings and you go home."

Turners Falls, where he began buying a complex of neighboring downtown buildings in recent years and made as his own home last fall, seems the perfect place for him, his work, his cathedral, whatever it finally turns out to be.

"This place started from struggle—with that darn Native American massacre—and it's sort of been struggling ever since. It's also a mill town, and the churches are decorated with, illustrated with, lots of biblical imagery and storytelling."

❊ ❊ ❊

Soon after his move to Turners Falls, the New York City stoneyard said it was cleaning up and offered de Christopher its limestone. He ordered six tractor-trailer loads—120 tons of limestone blocks—brought up to the village. He's been using that ever since. When he moved to a smaller K Street space in 2018, he gave it to a friend in Greenfield.

As heavy as the limestone is, there's an unmistakable lightness to many of de Christopher's stone carvings, which over the years have included loaves of bread, fishes, elephants, dogs, and bumbling, everyday humans—like those whose faces peer out from the windows of his 2017 Rock, Paper, Scissors paper factory. It's the same unabashed playfulness the artist uses to convert stories into sculpture.

"I'll be carving something, and I'll say, 'Oh look: There's a little guy!' And I carve the little guy. I'm very spontaneous sometimes with a material that's not all that spontaneous. I'll see a reflection of light from an angle and think, 'Oh, that looks like a nose in the shadow.'"

Unlike his fanciful napkin sketches, limestone "has its own demands and definitely changes as you make it. You have to make decisions all the way along as you're carving. It's the fragility of the stone: it doesn't have the molecular strength of granite. It's softer, a looser bind, and it's delicate. If you hit it the wrong way, it snaps off.

He's hoping to create a more secular imagery and tell a human story through his work. It's less the story of Turners Falls, as he'd thought at one point, than "scenes of human existence."

But if the *Cathedral Project* is de Christopher's "life's work, my opus magnus," it also requires a fund-raising effort that he can imagine undertaking. Other than grants he's received from the Leff and Berkshire Taconic Community foundations in 1999, de Christopher says, he hasn't solicited major grants.

"All I have to show right now are napkin drawings. I'm not a businessman, really."

At the 2001 Boston Flower Show, where he exhibited *The Elephant in the Blind Man's Garden,* he had a poster about the *Cathedral Project* that inspired a lot of people to toss coins into a fountain.

"I almost like that idea more than a huge sponsorship," he admits. "Cathedrals in days of old would raise a lot of money by getting shillings and two-pence tossed in their hats. They'd parade relics around and get donations."

But then again, it's a concept that's evolving as he gradually works on his properties—which include the designated site of the Turners Falls skate park between his new studio and his former workspace.

He bought his present studio because he wanted the closed-down skate park for his "cathedral." Now the town, which leases the skate park space, is considering re-establishing it.

He shrugs. Stay tuned.

And so his work, which has been exhibited at the DeCordova and the Norman Rockwell museums, emerges from stone. And he sees his *Cathedral Project* more abstractly, as the span of his career, "my works as expression of human spirit.

"I feel my way through these things, so they're constantly changing," the artist says, pointing to the face of *Shorty,* which has changed several times as he's carved. "I'll give the proviso to clients that what you see today is not what you'll see tomorrow."

That said, stone carving is a slow, reductive process that's not forgiving; once you've carved it, you can't undo what you've done. And so if the finished work already exists embedded in the stone, the carver simply teases it out.

"It's more like the work is in the artist," he says, "and I'm finding a way to draw that out of my own self."

Lucinda Brown,
restorative justice pioneer

Reinventing Justice

June 21, 2018

Because of its small size and the enlightened thinking of some lawyers and judges intent on seeing the antiquated legal system change to meet societal demands that by the 1990s was obvious to some, Franklin County became a laboratory for alternative approaches, including a restorative justice program. Overseen by a compassionate nonprofessional, Lucinda Brown, the program depended on volunteer panels to help offenders understand the impact their crime had on the community and then try to reconcile with victims. I served on one such panel. The following article marked Lucinda Brown's retirement. A portion is from a previous article published on May 9, 2012.

🔲 🔲 🔲

After robbing a convenience store where his friend worked, nineteen-year-old Tom Master had his case reviewed by one of ten or so Franklin County restorative probation boards, where five or six volunteers from the community heard about the crime from his point of view.

During multiple sessions over months, Master gradually began to discuss and think about the ways his crime had actually hurt people just like himself.

The store manager, who felt she'd unfairly lost her job because of that robbery, turned out to be a friend of his mother.

Ultimately, he and the clerk met in a group as part of the restorative probation process. When their session paused for a break, both of them stepped outside to get some fresh air, smoke a cigarette, and share a conversation.

As it was time to return, they hugged.

"It was phenomenal for me," says Master— his name changed for this story—about the overall process. "I was really in a desperate spot, and I made a wrong choice. I didn't do that kind of stuff. I didn't know what to do. I just had a newborn son. I didn't know what to do. Restorative probation just opened my eyes. I haven't been in trouble since. My life could have gone a totally different way."

He's one of about a thousand defendants who have gone through the region's restorative probation program, modeled after an approach used in the Yukon Territories and incorporated into the Franklin County Reinventing Justice process in 1998 to give defendants of nonviolent crimes a chance to understand their mistakes and learn from them.

Bringing the perpetrator back into the community to understand what they did and try to repair the situation isn't easy work. But the results can be profound.

"If you break the rules of a community, until you make amends, you're on the outside and have to earn your way back," explains Lucinda Brown. She trained with First Nation leaders from the Yukon Territory along with a presiding judge there and someone from the Minnesota Department of Corrections to set up the program here. Those indigenous leaders used a separation of time and space to give people who'd violated rules a chance to consider "Who am I? What's important to me? Who do I want to be? What are my values?" Brown says. "When they're ready to make amends, they could come back and become part of the community."

Brown, who began the restorative justice program nearly 20 years ago, is retiring after coordinating more than 150 volunteers and reviewing roughly 1,100 cases in as many as 20 settings around the county.

In the state's only program of its kind, Brown works with defendants referred by the courts as a condition of probation so the community's voice can help determine the outcome.

"I'm a one-of-a-kind animal," she says.

Because our legal system guarantees protections and rights to anyone accused of a crime, there's a system of "legal maneuvering," in her words, to safeguard civil liberties so that prosecutor and defense attorney become adversaries. Meanwhile, the defendant can avoid owning up to the harm done.

"The court is reactive, looking at what law was broken, whether it can be proven, and what's the punishment. It isn't about community or relationships. There are professionals speaking for those involved, the defendant definitely doesn't need to own responsibility, and they hear their lawyer minimizing what they did and the prosecutor demonizing what they did."

The process of casting a criminal case as state vs. so-and-so leaves the victim as a witness to the breaking of the law rather than thinking of trying to encourage the perpetrator to make amends. Victim and defendant are both removed from active participation in how the case is resolved. There's no teachable moment, no community healing, observes Brown.

"One of the pieces at the heart of the reinventing justice initiative is that the community would come to understand that together we have some responsibility for issues that come up that are community issues."

It's no surprise, for instance, that most of the young people who come through the program have failed in school, and many have had needs that have fallen through the cracks.

"Most people who come through the court don't feel part of the community, whatever that is. Many feel isolated, many are alienated from the mainstream, so why on earth would they follow the rules?"

In fact, many have felt victimized or harmed in some way, in school, in their families, but since nobody paid any attention to them, "their attitude is, 'Why should I care?' Is it any wonder they have an attitude about it?"

Brown guesses that about three thousand people have been victimized in the cases that have come before the nine boards. The process allows them to confront the defendant who, after layers of denial and self-defense, can genuinely open to hearing the story from the victim's point of view.

The system is far from perfect, admits Brown, who began volunteering for the overall Reinventing Justice program after working as a volunteer in the schools and watching how some students got into trouble. She saw them handed over to a justice system that made no timely connection between what they'd done and the consequences.

That's why the Franklin County Court Futures Task Force was created twenty-five years ago as a laboratory for mediation and other forms of "alternative dispute resolution" that would do more than decide guilt or innocence and mete out punishment. Brown volunteered in 1994 and was hired in 1995.

One problem she sees now is that the cases still have to wend their way through the court system. Another is in the makeup of volunteers, whose experience doesn't mirror that of those they're working with. "They're not people who work two or three jobs, who have no transportation. They're older, often from a different socio-economic status."

Yet, says Brown, "These are little steps. We often sow seeds."

▧ ▧ ▧

Many victims start out angry, but after they have a chance to feel that they've actually been listened to by a defendant who offers a sincere apology can advance to asking, "How do we make sure this doesn't happen again?"

Most of the cases are nonviolent. One involved a high school student charged with making a false fire alarm, malicious destruction of property, and trespassing stemming from an incident when he allegedly pulled a street signpost from the ground and climbed onto a school roof, waiting for firefighters to catch up with him.

In another, an eighteen-year-old and a friend, after drinking, broke into several vehicles, vandalizing them and stealing their contents, then throwing furniture off a porch and ripping a mailbox off a house.

For some defendants, it may be the first time in their lives they feel people are actually listening to what they say.

Often there's a web of issues they've been involved in, and the board is able to offer a way to look at them from a different perspective with hope for change.

At the panel's last meeting with one young woman, her mother was present to reflect on the help her daughter had been given. The mother asked the volunteers, "Where can I get the same kind of help?"

Master, who went on to volunteer on a restorative probation board himself, was able to get his high school equivalency diploma and then work at for a local manufacturer for several years.

After watching the store manager he'd befriended later die of a heart attack he now reflects, "I thank God I was able to make amends with her before it was too late. She understood where I was at the time, and she forgave me. I realized after what happened (that) I'd made a mistake, and I wanted to do everything to maintain a good life."

❉ ❉ ❉

As for Brown, she says, "My role is to create a good process and then keep that safe container to create the place for those conversations. If you create the good process, you'll get to a good place. The guidelines are to speak honestly and from your heart, listen to the person who's speaking, give everybody a chance to speak, and be respectful of others."

She calls Franklin County the stone soup center of the universe, and explains, "We're accustomed to not having all the resources we need, we're used to sharing, we're used to collaborating. That's how we survive. If we were able to look at all the reasons we should do this instead of all the reasons not to, it's absolutely possible, and the benefits are huge."

Instead of the innocent-until-proven-guilty principle, which leaves some defendants initially bewildered about admitting to themselves what they've actually done to someone, Brown says, "A true justice system would put the people harmed front and center and find ways to make them whole. The obligation of the person responsible would come second. What we've found is that the people responsible for wrongdoing often have been victimized themselves, and no one's supported them through that experience."

A casual observer of one of the sessions "might think this is just soft on crime, enabling people," she acknowledges. "But you can't expect empathy from someone who's never received empathy. Sometimes you have to go back and listen to that individual's story and unpack that to have them think about what would have helped them feel better and have community members say, 'You shouldn't have had to go through that.' That ends up being a very powerful turning point for many. Once you're there, you can work with them to work with the person who's been harmed to say, 'What's going to make this better for you?'"

Unlike vandalism, graffiti, and property-damage cases that dominated the program's early years, the more recent opioid crisis has yielded more "crimes motivated by desperation," in Brown's words: credit card larceny, identity theft, breaking and entering as well as possession of illegal substances.

"Those cases don't lend themselves to restorative justice in the court's time frame," she said. "There's a healing process people have to go through, getting off medication. It takes a long time for brains to heal, for people to start to feel things again. You can't ask people to have empathy if they're not able to do that yet."

photo by Peter Vallance

Dr. Kathy Bullock leads a workshop at Findhorn in Scotland .

Caught in the Spirit of Gospel

February 24, 2011

This was a feature story that grew out of my own interest in choral singing and was written as a first-person account of a workshop I attended at Rowe Conference Center with Kathy Bullock, a phenomenal gospel choral director I've enjoyed singing with numerous times. Especially since her retirement from Berea College, she's traveled the world offering choral workshops.

❋ ❋ ❋

Kathy Bullock appears suddenly in Rowe's rural, winter wonderland setting like the majestic being that she is.

Six feet, two inches tall, her chocolate-brown face contrasting against white snow as she descends the hill path in a long brown-and-tan West African mud cloth dress, her black hair twisted down to her shoulders. The apparition breaks into a gleaming smile as our group of nearly forty stands cheering from inside the breakfast hall at the first sight of our weekend workshop leader.

You'd think the beaming figure was a rock star, but towering Kathy Bullock —the head of Berea College's music department —is as down-to-earth as you can get.

A half dozen or so of us are from Greenfield Harmony chorus or River Singers, our Vermont sister choir, and had worked with

121

this choral leader before. Some sang in a recent weeklong Village Harmony singing camp in nearby Ashfield, and six others were from a Maine choral group that's worked with her. Others among us have only recently dared sing beyond our cars or showers.

This Singing in the Spirit: Gospel Music in Story and Sound workshop at Rowe Conference Center is offered just in time for Black History Month. Yet nearly all the participants are white but feeling the need to sing music of the African-American religious tradition simply because the sound moves us.

In fact, though we'll be singing gospel, several of us are Jewish so might even struggle with the notion of singing about—much less praising—Jesus.

Yet the weekend, we're about to learn, is about much more than music. Some who've worked before with the woman we'll all come to affectionately call Kathy already know that.

Kathy Bullock, I come to learn, is a force of nature like an energy-charged supernova. She can light up a room just by entering with an informal, "Hi, y'all." Literally within five minutes, she can get any group, regardless of race, age, or disposition rocking and reeling in song so that we're feeling like—though not necessarily sounding anywhere near as good as—the Edwin Hawkins Singers belting out, "Oh, Happy Day!"

John Bos of Shelburne Falls, one of only three men in our workshop, calls her "one of the few people in the world who shows me what the world can be."

Ricki Carroll of Ashfield, who's played host to Village Harmony singing camps with Bullock, describes the gospel leader as "love personified. She infuses life into everyone she meets."

We're about to experience the phenomenon for ourselves.

Without introduction from the upright piano in the rec hall, her hefty hiking boots hitting the pedals and her long fingers striking chords on the keys, Bullock launches us into song:

"You are welcome in this place."

It's a clear, simple, calming tune with straightforward lyrics, and suddenly we're all singing and know we're home.

"It's a blessing just to be here," she sighs, before summarizing what are characteristics of traditional Afro-American music: call and response, swaying movement, complex rhythms, syncopation, clapping, foot stomping and other upbeat percussion, celebration and praise. But the towering woman sets aside the list she'd made and explains about traditional African culture, gleaned from repeated visits to that continent to lead workshops.

"Music is part of our life, from the time you wake up to the time you go to sleep," says Bullock, who periodically leads singing tours to West Africa. The singing is functional: a song for grinding corn, for fishing, for going to war, for returning from war.

"It's just a simple part of life," so some African cultures don't even have a word for music as a separate art form. "Music is part of everything. It's not like you sit and watch or listen. It's a participatory kind of thing."

The core idea of singing as joining us together in community becomes absolutely clear a few minutes later when her simple request for someone to sing a solo line is met with frozen silence. Our characteristic New England restraint is spotlighted—uncomfortably.

"Some of you have voices that are more developed than others," Bullock responds matter of factly, like a very tactful mother. "But if you go back to the African world view, everybody sings. If you can speak, you sing. If you can walk, you dance. Now, somebody might do it a little differently from you, but only you can sing your song. In that tradition, if you say, 'I can't sing,' you're saying, 'I do not exist.' So feel free in a community of folks who share together and combine our voices."

If her invitation isn't crystal clear to us in our isolating earbud era of passive listening to celebrity singing, Bullock adds, "You are critical to the whole. You are valuable. Every one of us has a story only we can sing."

Magically, the ice has melted, and one woman volunteers to sing a solo line.

None of us have any doubt that Bullock's message—seemingly pivotal to our times—is as genuine as her voice. She is so grounded in believing what she says that we're instantly convinced.

But African communities were torn apart by the slave trade. "The people who were enslaved knew their lives didn't matter from one day to the next," she says. To make sense of their lives, they sang.

And in a powerful voice that scoops up energy from the large room, launching from the low floor and soaring to the high ceiling, Bullock resounds in a sweeping solo from a classic spiritual:

I am a poor pilgrim of sorrow.
I'm tossed in this wide world alone.
No hope I have for tomorrow . . .
Sometimes I am tossed and driven, Lord.
Sometimes I don't know where to roam.
I've heard of a city called heaven.
I've started to make it my home.

These are "sorrow songs," spirituals, Kathy explains to her hushed audience.

"People needed to make sense of a confusing and terrifying environment. They needed a way to find a sense of hope in a place where the law said they weren't even human. They needed to find a way to be. They sang their hope, their joy, their sorrow, their pain, their lives."

She quotes a teaching from Bernice Reagon of Sweet Honey in the Rock: "Music changes your condition."

"Immediately by singing, I'm no longer alone," says Bullock. "I become part of a collective. There's a sense of belonging. So all the spirituals are filled with hope. There's sorrow, but they're not sad."

❂ ❂ ❂

The cold, icy world beyond the windows silhouetting this woman as she speaks from the heart is a reminder that we, too, need hope, light, and each other.

A half-read email in our tote bag that day from Doug Wilson, the Unitarian minister who's director of the conference center, describes the darkness beyond our singing sanctuary: climate change, endless wars, joblessness, looming cuts to education and human services.

Yet if there's alienation in our dehumanizing era, there's also power in singing together, as we are, a gospel song that repeats simply:

"Thank you, Lord! Thank you for one more day!"

As someone who's lived my life as it comes, it seems a foreign concept to step back and discover a genuine power of profound gratitude. Only a devout atheist could reject outright such a declaration of life's magic. It seems especially meaningful that the song's expression has been handed down by a culture that's never known what tomorrow would bring.

One woman in our group, from Camden, Maine, who grew up singing songs of praise as an Orthodox Jew, tells us, "As I became more aware in my life, I became a lot more offended by the content of that music, because it wasn't just 'praise God,' but it was like, we're so terrible.

"It's really, really powerful to recognize how freeing it is to be able to sing this music and to move my body to it and not be in this restrictive situation where there're all these rules and 'thou shalt nots' and 'you can't do this,' and 'God's going to punish you' stuff. This is like, 'God is generous.' And it's not exclusive. You don't know how oppressive it is to be raised with that sense of isolation in the name of exclusivity."

She tells Bullock, "I'm just really grateful for the way you bring this with such an open heart and inclusiveness."

❀ ❀ ❀

Together we sing an impossibly upbeat song:
"I'm looking for a miracle!
I expect the impossible!
I feel the intangible!
I see the invisible!
The sky is the limit to what I can have!
Just believe and receive it, God will perform it today!"
A universal sense of hope and affirmation is embedded in Afro-American songs like "This Little Light of Mine," which took on new form and meaning as times changed, our workshop leader tells us. The blues emerged around the turn of the twentieth century and then gospel in the 1930s. Many in our group grew up hearing Freedom Songs of the 1960s along with funky Motown rhythms. Those Freedom Songs piggybacked onto spirituals, with their Old Testament references and allusions to an afterlife referring to liberation from tyranny.

"They come out of life. People sang them as they needed them, to be uplifted," explains Bullock, who grew up as one of six children of a Baptist minister in Washington, DC, "singing gospel as long as I can remember" in choirs and with her sisters. She studied piano and later flute. She arrived at Brandeis University to study psychology and linguistics, but found herself drawn back to music.

"Now more than ever," she insists, there's a crying need for these songs of liberation as a bridge to people who feel marginalized, downtrodden, disconnected.

Before she moved from Washington to rural Kentucky in 1991, Kathy Bullock's strongest wish was that she'd see her son live to be twenty-one, because the death rate among young urban Blacks is simply staggering.

"Half of the people I went to school with in the city are either dead or in jail," she says.

"Everywhere I go, people are hungry for an opportunity to connect and to share with one another more heartfelt things that come when you sing together and become a community."

Kathy Bullock makes no apology for the fact that the songs are rooted in Christianity, but she tries to find those that speak to a more ecumenical population.

"I come from the perspective and tradition of my Christian faith," she says. And yet, "The music is free. Take all you need, all you want. You can take it and engage in it how you will."

Those songs—old and new, often with multiple layers of meaning—carry a message of affirmation, a compassionate alternative to despair. One, written just after Hurricane Katrina, says,

You might be hurting, you might be crying,
You might be worrying and frustrated too.
Let me encourage you. Let me speak life to you.
You can depend on God to see you through.
I pray for you, you pray for me.
And watch God change things."

❖ ❖ ❖

If Bullock, always emphasizing community over ego, helps us find any beauty in our own individual voices by the end of the weekend, the singers eagerly, authentically shine the light back on her.

"She's an enabler," says Walter Cudnohufsky, who's returned to sing with Bullock several times. "She really allows you to go places you don't think you can go. She has passion. It's kind of an embodiment of the music, in a way."

Prue Berry, a former co-director of the retreat center, tells her, "You are a master of transmitting these songs to us in a way that allows us to feel and invite our own best selves to whatever we're doing. This is one of the best ways to take in music I've ever experienced. It's just as sweet as it can be."

Another participant, JoAnne Spies, says, "I feel like a whole code of ethics was presented: how to say what we need, how to depend on

God. So much was given to us, it's like if we listened, we learned how to live and how to be more truthful."

One woman, seated next to her wife, is close to tears as she says, as "part of a Southern-roots Pentecostal church, I sang that real heartfelt, spiritual deep Jesus stuff. And I sang it from a place of truth for me at that time. And I really can't do that anymore. Over the years, I've developed a new spirituality that's still within the Christian tradition, but it's way broader than that."

Kathy Bullock's explanation of how slaves brought singing with them from Africa and allowed it to evolve as life changed, the woman says, has given her the key to taking this uplifting music with her into her own, changed life.

"I can sing it again with who I am now. It's like I've been enslaved in my own life around the singing of gospel. And now I'm free."

**Len Weeks presides at Tire Warehouse,
Greenfield, Massachusetts**

The Zen of Len, Tires, and Timelessness

December 6, 2010

A ritual of winter in New England is changing to snow tires at the beginning and end of winter, which makes tire dealers ultra-popular destinations as the season of snowy weather approaches. But a palpable calm pervades one Greenfield tire shop despite lines of customers who turn out to get outfitted. It's a place with a decidedly mellow groove, thanks to owner Lenny Weeks. It just begged to be written about.

❈ ❈ ❈

Somewhere out in the Universe exists one of those shake-up snow globes with a miniature figure inside showing Tire Warehouse owner Lenny Weeks calmly handling the flurry of customers that crowd his waiting room for the annual ritual of changing over to snow tires.

Someone will probably present it to Weeks to display in his Federal Street store along with all of the Buddhas and peaceful paraphernalia that make Weeks's shop unlike any other auto service business this side of Katmandu.

Sandwiched between McDonald's and a Sunoco station, Tire Warehouse in Greenfield is outfitted with Buddhas indoors and out as well as flourishing bamboo and a tropical ficus tree plus a re-circulating fountain that looks like it might have been welded together from old tire irons, and an artificial aquarium with swimming jellyfish.

For those who notice, there are even crystals dangling around the store as well as hand-painted tires hanging outside.

All is calming. And then there's reality.

Customers start showing up at about 7 a.m. on Black Friday. By 7:30, when Weeks shows up, all six bays are filled with vehicles being outfitted for snow tires.

"We busted 'em out of here," Weeks explains during a lull about an hour later. "We're really efficient."

Manager Ken Lenois, stationed behind the work area, shakes his head. "What's tough about this business is you can't predict when we'll be busy."

Sort of like the first heavy snowfall, which is what typically drives customers to begin lining up in droves to have their studded snows put on.

"Wednesday, we were slammed with people wanting to change 'em over," says Lenois, because many knew they'd be traveling for Thanksgiving and there had been forecasts of rain mixed with sleet for Black Friday.

Despite Weather Channel's focus on "severe weather" out West and forecasts that include possible snow headed our way, Black Friday's tire customers are either early birds who want to beat the rush or who have unpredictable tire needs.

"I expected to see a mob in here," says Bill Dornbusch of Colrain, who shows up to get his snow tires changed over "'cause you never know. In Colrain, it's a good thing to get them on beforehand. Last year, I was late and waited for the first snow day. I had to wait a couple of hours."

Weeks says there's no business like snow business, which probably represents from fifteen to twenty percent of overall Tire Warehouse transactions.

"It usually comes on very rapidly with the first snowstorm. And for the first three or four snowstorms, we're very, very busy," he says in a soft-spoken, calming voice that sets the tone for his third-generation family business.

That's appreciated by customers like Alan Bristol of Erving, who shows up with a flat he got while driving to his family's Thanksgiving dinner in Greenfield.

"We slid off the highway," says Bristol, who remembers first coming to Weeks's business with his family when he was a kid and now brings in his own kids because they love the bamboo and oddball touches, like the blue electrostatic lighted globe held up by a small Buddha on the counter.

※ ※ ※

"I don't go to many other shops, but I do think it's a little different here," admits Weeks, adding that it's his sister, Charlotte, who's Buddhist and not him. So the Buddhas "just kind of find their way here. We don't know why or how, but it's a nice way to look at things. We have a little fountain that runs water, and it's pretty soothing. Because we do get a little crazy and stressed out. So we find a way to meet it."

There are some other oddball calming elements around the store, like a large painting hanging over the customer counter that shows Weeks himself sitting cross-legged on the floor happily playing hand drums. Overhead, there's a giant sun-like tire decked out with candles. Below is the awning over the shop's bays, where Weeks's employees are depicted working on cars.

The painting, by area artist Nina Rossi, is framed by four aphorisms—the kind that Weeks' wife, Susan, contributes to the ever-changing sign that captures people's attention along Federal Street: "No rain, no rainbows." "Now is the moment of power." "Faith celebrates the miracle." "Everything works out perfectly."

Often the sign offers a thought-provoking inspiration like, "Imagination is more important than knowledge. Tell your kids."

"We get a comment every single day about the sign," Weeks says. "Most of it's about philosophy or healing. Much of it's just to send out a healing message. We sort of carry the torch just to believe it's a good world."

That torch also glows inside the business, which Wilder Weeks, Len's grandfather, started in 1950 as Weeks Firestone. It sold appliances as well as tires, but when Len's father, Wilder Leon Weeks, took over in 1985, he dropped the appliance line and the retread business and called it Tire Emporium.

Lenny Weeks, who joined the business at age sixteen on Saturdays to help pay his way through the University of Massachusetts studying psychology and then environmental science, took over in 1989 and changed the business to Tire Warehouse, ending the auto repairs they'd done there. Len's son Jarad also works there.

The fifty-seven-year-old owner, who with his wife has studied clairvoyance, trained with a shaman for five years and then spent four or five years learning Native American healing using the essence of plants, admits "I'm sort of spiritual," and the nine crystals that hang around the store are part of his wife's study of the Chinese philosophy of feng shui, adding to the slightly mystical mood of Tire Warehouse.

For a while, Weeks tried out his healing studies directly on customers, offering to check the pressure of their wrists along with their tire pressure, "because that was part of my training. People really liked it. It was just a little unusual."

Along with keeping his sense of humor in the high-stress business, Weeks says, "We kind of take everything in stride. I really give gratitude to whatever is: the town, the people. We're very blessed. We try to keep our spirit up here and bring other people's spirits up."

And so every customer receives a pink or red carnation along with their receipt.

"Besides saying 'Thank you for your business,' it's something that says we really mean it. A lot of times, a guy doesn't know what to do with it. He's embarrassed because no one's ever given him a flower. Then before you know it, people start telling you their life's story. It's like *Siddhartha*. For years he transported people across the river. So we get a little bunch of everybody's history really quickly. A lot of times, it's about death or dying, so we have a little poem we pass out to them about sailing ships."

For Weeks, adding little spiritual touches to a wrenching business "keeps me sane. If I just did the business, I would burn out. But these other things bring light and renewing energy."

For Weeks's eight or nine employees, there's a calming influence, too.

"They sort of know it and feel it," he says. "We talk about stuff if they've got problems. Someone once described my business as a Buddhist finishing school for wayward pirates. A lot of these guys, they've had a tough family life and need a place to have respect. I love these guys. It's a great crew."

One worker once mistakenly told a customer the store didn't have a particular tire. His light-hearted punishment was to have to write "No one walks" a hundred times on a small chalkboard that hangs in the back room.

Weeks also brought his crew to the town common to clean up at one point, and he's hoping to bring them to cut limbs that obscure the billboard welcoming traffic to town along the interstate.

He says he's always thinking about ways to welcome his customers.

"It's like home. We spend more time here than we do with our families. It's because we have a relaxed attitude that my help works so hard. Life is too short to be serious and all business."

Contra dancers in Guiding Star Grange Hall, Greenfield, Massachusetts, include Ted Renaud, center, wearing a Georgetown University sweatshirt

Breaking the Sound Barrier on the Contra Line

December 2, 2013

Greenfield is a magnet for contradancers, with multiple dances vibrating the floorboards at the Guiding Star Grange Hall multiple times each week. The revival came just a few years after 1976 when I arrived already primed for the traditional New England dance form. As a dancer, I wrote several features about what the resurgence was about, but I became especially intrigued when I learned that one dancer couldn't hear the live music that had us enthralled as we stomped and swung. An interpreter assisted me with this interview.

※ ※ ※

Ted Renaud swings. He balances. He turns with his partner. He dances up and down the contra line along with other enthusiasts from around the region and sometimes around the country who fill Greenfield's Guiding Star Grange on Fridays and Saturdays.

In fact, Renaud steps in line four or five times most weeks, traveling to dances in Amherst as well. And, oh, even at dawn dances that last right until 7 a.m., living it up and getting down with all the zeal of the other regulars drawn by the music and the down-home fun.

Yet Renaud is completely deaf.

He can't hear the intricate, mesmerizing music of Wild Asparagus or the fiddling or the contra-dance calls of David Kaynor. He can't easily pick up on the cues of bassist Stu Kenney, flutist David Cantini, or pianist Anne Percival changing the tune, can't hear whether it's an exuberant jig or a high-flying reel he's moving to with scores of other dancers.

But Renaud, 63, loves his silent contra dances just the same.

The longtime resident and native of Greenfield can tell when the tempo or the energy level has picked up. And he's often able to tell other dancers when they're messing up because they weren't listening to what the caller said.

"'Huh? How'd you know that if you're deaf?' I get asked all the time," Renaud says through an interpreter, who at times has accompanied him to dances.

Most of the time, though, he's on his own, stepping up between dances to a prospective partner and prancing two right-hand fingers over his open left palm, then extending them as a clear, unspoken invitation: "Come, dance?"

Renaud worked in Greenfield for decades— doing janitorial work at the YMCA, at the Greenfield *Recorder*, at the Garden Theater when grand murals still adorned its walls. He knew that contra dances were drawing lots of people to the Grange but didn't discover those dances for himself until he dared to walk in about four years ago.

"The first time, I sat there and just watched and took it all in," he says using sign language that he learned first at the American School for the Deaf in Hartford, Connecticut, birthplace of American Sign Language, and then at the Austine School for the Deaf in Brattleboro, Vermont.

Born hearing, Renaud was just a few months old when an untreated ear infection made him deaf.

Around him at the Guiding Star, he can see a sea of people moving joyfully to intricate rhythms and melodies that he can only try to imagine. But he's been used to that sense of separation for decades, he explains.

At that first dance, "A woman tapped me on the shoulder and asked, 'Do you want to dance?' I tried it, and I made lot of mistakes. Then I sat, and I watched some more. Little by little, I tried all the dances. They kept asking me to dance, so I went out on the floor."

With the help of some patient women and men as well, he explains, "Now I don't worry about it."

Renaud, who's always been athletic and loved playing basketball until recently, works out regularly at the gym. He says that dancing provides great exercise. "This is my new sport," he jokes, especially since years of enthusiastically participating in athletics has left parts of his body aching.

It's also great exercise for his mind. It's a mind that's long used visual cues as strong compensation for an inability to hear.

"I just watch what everybody is doing. I can't hear a thing," says Renaud, a skilled woodworker who examines so carefully how a piece of furniture is made that he can go home and duplicate it, as he once did when he needed a gift for his daughter, measuring in his mind something that had caught his eye at Andy's Pine Shop.

"Dancing is the same way. If people stop, I stop. All with my eyes."

"Everyone asks, 'How can you dance if you can't hear anything?' My eyes have become my ears."

After four years, some dancers have taken notice of this dancer in his white shoes who fits in so seamlessly in the contra line that you might not even know he can't hear.

"He's a wonderful dancer," says Mary Jones of Turners Falls, who's seen Renaud week after week at English country dance sessions in Amherst and has encountered him at contra dances as well. "A lot of contra-dance callers have had no idea he's deaf. He watches carefully, and he's very, very good with short-term memory. You go through the dance once or twice, and he knows what the patterns are."

Mimicking is one thing, but Renaud also keeps his wits about him in a jumping Grange that's cloister silent for him, whether Becky Tracy or Van Kaynor is fiddling or Steve Zakon-Anderson is calling. It's the ultimate social situation for someone for whom life could be isolating. "You have to change partners all night, so you're meeting lots of people."

But it's not necessarily a breeze. He's watched four deaf friends come to dance only to be scared off by how mixed up they got and how difficult it was for them to get the hang of what they were doing. They gave up, but Renaud takes pride in the fact that he stuck with it.

"My attitude when I first started dancing was, 'I can do it,'" recalls Renaud, who makes sure he gets to special dances in Peterborough,

New Hampshire or the all-night Brattleboro, Vermont, dawn dances or Dance Flurry in Saratoga, New York.

"Contradancing can get rough and fast. Fast, fast, fast—pushing and pulling and twisting and turning and spinning. You have to use light hands so your partner doesn't get injured." Renaud sometimes finds himself close to getting slapped in the face by a spinning partner's ponytail. Sometimes, he adds, expressively with a panicked pace, "With chopsticks in her ponytail!"

English country dancing, which Renaud enjoys going to weekly, is graceful, often slower and more difficult, although there, too, the other dancers are helpful.

Sometimes, though, it's Renaud—undistracted by the music or the chatter of people around him—who comes to the aid of other, more befuddled dancers.

Balding, smiling, Renaud doesn't necessarily know terminology like "balance and swing" or "hay," but then, those words also don't get in the way of him showing a wayward dancer with gestures to "go there and spin."

That happens plenty at Wednesday night dances in Amherst, where many of the dancers are students who are first timers at contras.

"They want me to teach them," he says as he gestures dramatically how he tried to convey the absurdity of the situation. "'I'm deaf. I can't do it! You're hearing. you can do it!' They're stuck in one spot. I can't turn them around."

Still, while he can't hear the tunes, Renaud can often feel pulsing vibrations from the dance floor, thanks to enthusiastic dancers who kick up their heels in a steady tempo or bang the floor accenting a balance, swing, or step here or there.

"It helps me dance," he admits.

If there are drums, as there sometimes are, Renaud can feel those as vibrations in his chest. But when there are mainly fiddles and keyboards and no musical vibrations—as with waltzes—he depends on the guidance of partners.

"It was mind-boggling," he says of his first encounter with a waltz in its three-four meter. He's had help with partners who have tapped out the rhythm on his back, and now he loves waltzing.

"A few people know the basics of sign language," and he'll write his name for them on his hand. On the sole of his black-and-white shoe, he's written, "Hi. I'm Ted."

"It is difficult for me in a hearing world. And I do feel isolated and left out, cut off," Renaud admits. "But I have lived in this world sixty-three years, and this is normal for my life. Often, there are people at the dances who know a little sign language, and I'm really lucky that there are a couple ladies who can actually interpret for me. I am very grateful for their help, and everyone who makes the effort to communicate with me in sign language helps me to feel a little less isolated."

Dancing is not only good exercise, Renaud says. It's also good therapy.

"It's a lot of fun. There's a lot of smiling."

Mary Leue pauses from work in her garden.

Dreams of a Real Community

July 1, 2017

I only met Mary Leue once, but when I did, she was a truly memorable character: spunky, sharp, full of wit, and more accomplished than I'll ever be. During editing of Flights of Fancy, Mary is 103. And still living at home with family close by. A remarkable woman, by anyone's measure.

▨ ▨ ▨

Mary Leue of Ashfield reaches back easily into her spry ninety-seven-year-old head to pull out a couple of memories of growing up in her family of six children in a suburb west of Boston.

"My father was busy as an ob-gyn and was gone most of time. My mother realized we needed freedom. She used to let me go, and I'd run barefoot all over town."

Leue is seated at the kitchen table on a morning chilly enough to keep a fire going in the woodstove at the Cape Street house her mother discovered with a girlfriend after a long horse-and-buggy ride in 1908. There are shelves crammed with books, and her iPad, on which she'd been playing mah jong a few minutes earlier, is in front of her.

She launches into another vivid memory. It's about the first-grade schooling she received from her grandmother, who'd been a teacher years earlier, at a point when the family was moving from one town to another.

"She let me do what I wanted to do, and I just grew by leaps and bounds," says Leue, whose greatest claim to fame is creating the Albany Free School in 1969. "I realized kids don't need all this repetition, like lock-step learning, where you can't learn about adjectives until you've learned about verbs, and whatever."

Ever a free spirit, Leue recalls seizing the opportunity to set up what today claims to be "the oldest independent inner-city alternative school in the United States."

The idea for the school fell into place after the youngest of her five children came home hating his fifth-grade experience—"a mix of boredom, anonymity, and curricular oppression on the part of his teacher, who was fixated on long division both for homework and the following morning's classwork every day," according to Leue's three-volume published memoir.

"Mark's teacher was over retirement age, and she was very cranky," Leue recalls. "Mark said to me, 'You can teach. Let me stay home, and you can teach me. She's just awful.'"

Leue had gotten her undergraduate degree at Bryn Mawr, followed by a nursing degree, and after working on a master's in psychology at Texas Women's University, she continued graduate studies at the State University of New York at Albany—with a lot of frustration.

As someone who had loved studying Freud and Jung while in Texas, Leue found that at SUNY, "They were gung-ho rat psychologists. I couldn't stand it! They were focused on statistics, and I hate statistics!"

Rather than run their maze, "I fought with it. I had had my elegant designs for a thesis. I wanted to do something in education. I had a lovely program to balance boy, girl, mother, father, which was more influential.

"'No! You can't do that!'

"So I quit. Who needs it? Who wants it?"

She'd taught in Texas, tutored in Maine, and done religious education work at the Unitarian church in Albany, where her Harvard-trained husband was teaching philosophy at the state university in 1961. After returning from her husband's sabbatical year in England, their ten-year-old son, Mark, was encouraging her to run free once more.

Leue launched into home schooling Mark—who now lives nearby. Lessons included for the first Earth Day in 1970 collecting twenty bags of garbage from an embankment. They also included helping out at a day-care center, putting on plays, learning to develop film and making movies, plus cooking and baking.

Soon after she began, a friend asked if Leue could teach three of her children as well.

"I said, 'I've got to go on with this.'"

Leue had learned from a Schenectady minister about Summerhill, the alternative boarding school in England set up less than two years after her birth. After reading about the original free school and corresponding with its founder, A. S. Neill, "I decided I wanted to start a school like Summerhill in downtown Albany. It just seemed like the right way to teach kids."

Neill responded to Leue's idea of establishing an inner-city free school in this country, "I would think myself daft to try!"

Her school—which emphasized that student families could pay just what they could afford and cook, clean, or otherwise help out— grew. She founded the Free School in 1969.

"Kids kept coming by asking, 'What you doing here? This is a school? Can I come?'" Leue recalls.

"Gradually, I accumulated more and more kids from the neighborhood," which had recently become an African-American ghetto. "At the same time, SUNY faculty members who heard about the school asked for their kids to come. We developed a really nice mix. It was very lively. We had a really nifty, wild school."

One hurdle had been convincing school officials to let her run with her plans. Yet, she found a friend in Albany Education Department's head, who became a strong supporter of the school she built in her home.

"We used to have pie nights. We would sell pie and would have a big dinner with a pie auction. He always came."

And as it blossomed, the school outgrew her home. Leue, using money her mother had left her, gradually bought an old, former church building.

Eventually, she bought several abandoned buildings in the South End neighborhood at auction, including an old barn and a four-story tenement—in part to house staff who were attracted from around the country. There were also teaching interns from Antioch University in Keene, New Hampshire, as suggested by her son Tom, who was studying there and now also lives nearby.

"We'd go bid and were often the only bidders," Leue says. "And we'd get it for free."

❊ ❊ ❊

Mary Macomber Leue, two and a half years shy of a century, admits that trying to remember recent events isn't so good. But when it comes to recalling episodes from years ago, there's little stopping her.

At nine, she recalls, "My father outfitted a Model A Ford truck with iron hoops in the bed and a canvas cover with roll-up windows to keep the rain out. And boards to stretch across as seats."

All six kids headed out West with her parents and godmother, her mother's friend Bucky Freeman, for a camping trip just before the Great Depression.

"I'll never forget. We went through Canada on gravel roads. It was just a terrible racket all the way west to Alberta and British Columbia. But it was spectacular scenery, and the Canadians had very good tourist camps."

Leue remembers her brothers' fights along the way and "the way Bucky kept us from fighting, because the twins were always punching each other and teasing the girls—was she told us stories. She was a wonderful storyteller and told us about Birdseed, who was a boy, and his friend, a pirate named Squint Eye. The adventures of Birdseed and Squint Eye just poured out of her. She was amazing."

Her mother and Bucky, a Smith College theater professor with whom she had an intimate relationship, had come upon the Ashfield house they named Journey's End after a long buggy ride from Northampton and bought it, with a hundred surrounding acres, for five hundred dollars. The house, which they had restored as a family getaway as well as a summer farm camp for young working girls from Boston, also holds fond memories of Leue's own visits as "the high point of my summer" growing up.

When she was fourteen, her father invited her one day to come along while he was seeing patients at Massachusetts General Hospital.

141

"Here I was in his Ford V-8, sitting at the curb in the summertime, and it went on for a long time. I went into the glove compartment, and there was this booklet, 'How to Drive a Ford.' So I taught myself to drive just sitting there several hundred times waiting for him."

Later on, when Bucky asked her to come with her out to Ashfield, Leue told her, "I can drive!" So her godmother got out and let her drive all the way from Framingham to Ashfield.

"I'd never driven on a real road before," she says with a laugh. "I've got nerve. I had no business doing any of that. I didn't lie to her. I just didn't tell her how I'd managed to learn."

❁ ❁ ❁

The Albany Free School still operates with about forty students ages two through fourteen, with a preschool component that Leue set up. "Like forty-eight years, by far the oldest in the country," Leue says.

It may be her greatest claim to fame, but it's not the only one.

Leue, who'd worked briefly as an obstetric and pediatric nurse in 1950 at Newton-Wellesley Hospital, went on to be a labor coach, childbirth educator, pregnancy and fertility consultant, and midwifery teacher twenty-five years later and founded a pregnancy and childbirth support group as part of the Family Life Center of Albany, today the longest standing independent childbirth support center in New York's Capital Region.

Jerry Mintz, a Vermont free-school founder who began working with Leue in the National Coalition of Alternative Community Schools in the 1970s and heads the Alternative Education Resource Organization, says, "She's a brilliant person who followed up on things we learned from people like Jonathan Kozol, such as that you don't just want to have a tuition-based school for rich kids."

Instead, Leue "organized a whole community of people who would fix up a building," Mintz says, "and eventually the rent money was used to keep the tuition very low so they could always have a sliding scale and a broad cross section of students."

The rental, for housing families and staff, helped generate 60 to seventy percent of the school's funding, according to former school co-director Chris Mercogliano.

"The seeds she planted then are bearing fruit now," says Mintz. Emphasizing learner-centered programs and democratic education principles, where students have a say in how the school is run, Leue's ideas about free education play out in charter schools and programs around the world where students are involved in setting policy and curriculum, in peer counseling, and even in teaching, he adds.

"We made it clear to people that the current system wasn't functioning," he says. "There are thousands of alternative schools all over the world still, and there are lots of democratic schools. It's a fast-growing movement. In Israel there are thirty public democratic schools."

But all wasn't roses.

Leue recalls, "Soon after we got organized with enough kids to make a difference, kids were coming to me with angry feelings, with unfinished business they had with other kids. She put up a blackboard at the school on what she called "the problem wall."

"When they came to me with something, I'd say, 'That sounds like a problem. Want me to write it on the wall for you?' As they became older, I'd say, 'Can you write it on the wall?' It made me realize how you could encourage kids to solve their own problems."

Later on, she encouraged students to form a problem-solving group and told them, "'I'd like to turn this problem over to you.' Whenever a kid came to me with a problem, I'd say, 'Have you called a council meeting yet?' They had a big bell, and the kid would run out of the room, saying, 'Council meeting!'"

Chris Mercogliano, who arrived in 1973 at the Free School with his then-girlfriend Betsy to teach, says, "Mary was an educational visionary who had a way of connecting with kids right on their level. She particularly knew how to read kids and could just see inside them and had an uncanny understanding what a kid needed in terms of their overall growth as human beings.

"She was extremely creative," he continues, "and would do magical things with kids, like go digging for buried treasure in the basement. Or we'd bring two dozen inner-city kids to her farm in Ashfield for a week at a time so they could open up to learning."

Leue, he says, often helped troubled kids who had been turned off from learning and had been labeled failures.

"Mary was just a genius at turning that whole thing around and having those kids fall in love with learning again. She really understood kids on an emotional level," says Mercogliano, who became co-director of the school after Leue left in 1985 and still volunteers there a couple of mornings a week.

She went on to help create a shared investment and loan program called the Money Game, a medically supported midwife-managed pregnancy, birth, and parenting initiative along with a weekly support panel, the Group, to help community members work through conflicts and build interpersonal skills as well as Adult Learning Exchange, a community adult-ed network. She created a publishing house and small bookstore, Down to Earth Books, along with a food co-op, the Down to Earth Store.

In 1985, after teaching herself web mastering, she began publishing and editing *SKOLE*, a journal of grass-roots alternative education. Then in 1995, she helped create the *Journal of Family Life,* and continued editing both publications until 1999. In addition to articles in national and international journals of education and psychotherapy, Leue has published twenty-seven Down-to-Earth books, including ten as author, seventeen as editor, and five as contributing author. Proceeds were plowed back into the free school, which also set up a two-hundred-acre outdoor education center in Grafton, New York.

The school is surrounded by the community of faculty and staff, students, their families and members of the inner-city neighborhood she built in what might be considered her greatest legacy.

"It's amazing how much we were able to do with very little money," Mercogliano says. "Another big piece of Mary's vision was people living together as a real community where everybody pitched in and did stuff together. She worked really hard to pull us all into that vision. It was a powerful thing" with everyone invested in volunteering and offering to train students in everything from cooking to flying a plane.

"The school's presence made an enormous difference in the neighborhood," says Mercogliano. He still lives there along with several of the core teachers who worked alongside Leue.

Most incredibly, he adds, "She never asked for a dime. Nada. She just did it, because she cared."

In 1985, when Leue moved back to Ashfield where she'd spent summers as a girl, she returned to gardening, which she had always loved. She also grew asparagus and planted apple seeds to start seedlings to transplant.

"Now they're bearing, and all of them had blossoms this spring," says Leue, showing appreciation for the uniqueness of every tree, just as she did with every child.

"Each one is different, so I have different names for them."

**A statue memorializes
Sojourner Truth, abolitionist, in
Florence, Massachusetts.**

photo by Richie Davis

Flights of Fancy Tour

October 18, 1997

*When you have the birthplace of Dr. Seuss just down the
road and you realize that Elsie the Cow and Johnny Appleseed
also considered this neck of the woods home, it doesn't take a
lot of imagination to dream up a whimsical travel feature like the
following. What it did take was a team of trusting editors who
allowed enough latitude for one of their few reporters to go off
for an afternoon or two in search of a somewhat elusive story.*

⊠ ⊠ ⊠

Tired of traveling with bus tours that leave you exhausted but
explore the same ol' same ol'?

Stumped by where to take your visiting relatives who've been
everywhere?

Hungry for something completely different?

Here it is. The Greenfield *Recorder's* Toura Obscura. Or: "Bet you never knew the Bay State had something for everyone."

There are at least two ways to enjoy this flights of fancy tour. One is to actually hop on your whim-sy-cle, grab your map, friends, and imagination, and leave yourselves plenty of time to explore other sites you happen to find along the way. If you don't have an entire day to spend, try spreading it over days.

There's also the virtual tour, which you can do right in your own home. After "visiting" each site, close your eyes and just imagine how each fits into its surroundings.

In researching this seeming tour-de-farce—which is for real—we purposely left out the obvious and tried to place the sites in some sort of geographic order for easy travel. The Emily Dickinson House in Amherst, the former home of Minute Tapioca in Orange, or Laughing Brook Wildlife Sanctuary in Hampden may be on plenty of other lists. But here's your chance to visit some less noted but still notable sites.

❦ ❦ ❦

Elsie the Cow—America's most famous lactress of all time—was a knockout Jersey whose real name was You'll Do, Lobelia. She won plenty of prizes for Elm Hill Farm in Brookfield before being spotted by an agent for Borden's and leased as the nation's Number 1 bovine superstar, dressed in an embroidered green blanket at the 1939 New York World's Fair.

By the time she died at age nine in a 1941 traffic accident, Elsie had appeared in an array of improbable places, from the bridal suite in New York's Waldorf Astoria to leaving her hoof prints at Hollywood's Grauman's Chinese Theater. She also appeared at the 1939 New York World's Fair and starred as Buttercup in the 1940 movie version of Louisa May Alcott's *Little Men*.

But everyone's favorite Jersey always came home to her 1,050-acre Brookfield farm on East Main Street, where she was best loved and is best remembered.

John Spencer, who worked on his grandparents' farm as a boy and still works on what is now a vegetable, horse, and sheep farm, even recalls when Elsie was photographed going up the steps of Brookfield Town Hall for a dance. Orlando Streeter, now in his mid eighties, still has a framed picture of Elsie to recall the days when he worked on the farm.

Elm Hill, with well-appointed barns and a splendid view of the surrounding countryside, was recently donated to the National Audubon Society as a wildlife sanctuary.

Speaking of Elsie Borden, there is, of course, in Fall River the home of Lizzie Borden, who is infamously accused of giving her father and stepmother forty and forty-one whacks with an ax, respectively, in 1892.

Closer to Elsie's old stall, though, is the well where Joshua Spooner was murdered and thrown into by three Revolutionary War soldiers at the urging of his wife, Bathsheba Spooner, on March 1, 1778. All four were executed in Worcester four months later. The well with a stone marker is less than a quarter-mile down the road from Elm Hill Farm.

⊞ ⊞ ⊞

Mary's Little Lamb lived in Sterling on what's now Route 62, north of Worcester.

Yes, there really was a Mary, who had a little lamb that really did follow her to school. The old Redstone Hill schoolhouse, on the road to Clinton, is no longer in Sterling, because Henry Ford had it moved in 1927 to Longfellow's Wayside Inn on Route 20 in Sudbury. But you can visit the lamb—or a stone facsimile thereof—on Sterling Town Common.

You can also see the homestead of Mary Elizabeth Sawyer (1806-1889) who became a matron at McLean Hospital in Belmont and who really was followed to school along with her brother Nathaniel in about 1815, according to a sixth-generation descendant of Nathaniel, Diane Malone. Malone, with her sister, owns the corner house on Maple Street, which runs just off the center of town, and is trying to have it restored with the help of the Mary Sawyer Foundation.

"I did not have many playmates outside the dumb creatures on the place," Mary Sawyer Taylor wrote in later years. "There were not many little girls to play with, and I had few dolls. But I used to dress up my lamb in pantalets, and had no end of pleasure in her company."

Taking the lamb to school, she wrote, was Nat's idea. Placed under her seat and covered with a blanket, the lamb reportedly rested quietly and was undiscovered until Mary went forward to recite. "There was a clatter, clatter, clatter on the floor, and I knew it was the pattering of the hoofs of my lamb."

All six stanzas of the rabid doggerel were included in McGuffey's old second-grade reader along with these study exercises: "What did Mary have? Where did the lamb go with Mary? What did the lamb do? Why did he love Mary? How can we make animals love us?"

The lamb, sent out of the classroom by teacher Rebecca Kimball and whose visit was recorded by one John Roulstone and later by Sarah Josepha Hale "to inculcate moral truths and virtuous sentiments," later gave birth to three lambs of her own and was gored to death by a cow when she was nearly four years old, according to an 1889 letter written by Mary.

※ ※ ※

John "Johnny Appleseed" Chapman was born in Leominster on September 26, 1774, one of three children of Nathaniel and Elizabeth Chapman. His birthplace is noted by a stone marker on Johnny Appleseed Lane off Mechanic Street near Route 2.

The suburban lane, complete with new homes, runs beside Route 190. The marker is surrounded by trees, not one of which is a fruit tree.

Johnny Appleseed, as he came to be known, was a practical nurseryman who saw a business opportunity in the westward migration and moved ahead of the pioneers to supply seeds and seedlings, starting nurseries throughout the Midwest.

Chapman appeared in Ohio by 1800, quoting from the Bible but not necessarily wearing an overturned saucepan for a cap, as Disney imagined. He owned many tracts of land throughout Ohio and Indiana and used this land to transplant seedlings and set out orchards.

※ ※ ※

Lake Chaubunagungamaug in Webster is commonly known as Lake Webster, and you can see why.

Locals refer to it as Lake Chargogg, and it makes any other American Indian place name pale by comparison. My map listed it as simply Lake Chaubunagungamaug, which is braver than Webster but a far cry from the forty-seven-letter name, which has been very loosely translated as, "You fish on your side, I fish on my side, Nobody fishes in the middle."

In fact, says eighty-nine-year-old Bertha Hart, the fourteen-syllable phrase is the combined name of the three Nipmuk bands that laid claim to different parts of the water body: the Chargoggagoggs, the Manchaugagoggs and the Chaubunagungungamauggs.

149

Hart, who grew up on the lake and is president of the Webster Historical Society, says her father hand-carved three signs that spell out the lake's native American name. One of those signs, several feet across, still hangs at the marina on Point Breeze. The name is also painted on a girder beneath Interstate 395 to welcome visitors entering Webster's Memorial Park.

The most endearing memory in this town along the Rhode Island border may be the Tin Pan Alley song that Blanche Fiddes used to sing with her fifth-grade classes at Webster Elementary School, written in 1935:

> Down beside the rippling water, it will set your heart agog,
> On Lake, Chargog-gagogg, manchaugagogg—chau-bun-a-gun-gungamaugg.

And the rhythm of the bullfrogs, with their lovelorn dialogue, at Lake, etc.

> Oh there is lots, oh such a lot to do, you lose all track of time,
> Nobody knows it's Sunday 'til you hear the church bells chime!

You can find out where this place is, if you look up your geog. It's Lake Char . . . (etc.)

▩ ▩ ▩

The Dr. Seuss House is not on Mulberry Street, as you might expect from the Seuss book title *To Think That I Saw it on Mulberry Street*, but on Fairfield Street in Springfield, just a block from Forest Park, where author Theodore "Seuss" Geisel's father was zookeeper.

The Springfield Library and Museums Association is planning a Seuss Sculpture Garden, but despite the fact that Seuss brought fame to Springfield's zoo ("*If I Ran the . . .*) and Mulberry Street, where his grandparents lived (*And to Think that I Saw It On . . .,*) there are precious few markers that point out he lived his early years here.

The exceptions, unmarked and privately owned, are the house at 74 Fairfield Street, the site of his birth, 22 Howard Street, and the stone at Oak Grove Cemetery off Bay Street, where his parents, Theodore and Henrietta, are buried.

> There are no signs that show the way,
> The house is there, not blue but gray.
> It's gray you say? The house that stands there to this day?
> At Oak Grove his folks are laid to rest,
> But Seuss, alas, lies way out west.
> Don't fret . . . sweat . . . regret! It's all for the best.

The city of Lowell remembers its native son Jack Kerouac. He was born on Lupine Road, is buried in Edson Cemetery, and even has his knapsack on display at the Lowell National Historic Park Working People's Museum.

Beat writer Kerouac is memorialized also in a commemorative park where excerpts from his spoken-language songs describing life in this Merrimack mill city are etched onto six granite columns beside the canal.

"The mystery of the Lowell night extends to the heart of downtown. It lurks in the shadows of the redbrick walls," he wrote in his autobiographical novel, *Dr. Sax.*

Lowell attracts hundreds of Kerouac fans each year, according to Mark Hemingway, president of Lowell Celebrates Kerouac. Walking tour maps are available at the national park visitor's center.

You can visit St. Jean Baptiste Church, called by Kerouac "the ponderous cathedral of the slums," where his funeral was held; Funeral Row, a series of funeral homes, including the one where his wake was held; Nicky's Bar on Gorham Street, where he hung out; and a 1911 replica of the Grotto at Lourdes, about which he wrote, "Everything there was to remind of Death, and nothing in praise of Life."

Each October, Lowell hosts a Kerouac festival, and this year's festival was complemented by a photo exhibit at the Whistler House Museum of Art. The museum, the birthplace of the nineteenth-century painter James McNeill Whistler, is, like the park, an attraction in itself.

If you go, advises Hemingway, make sure you've read "Dr. Sax" first. "It's all right here!"

❀ ❀ ❀

Cal Coolidge, the laconic lawyer whose path led from Plymouth, Vermont, through Amherst and Northampton on his way to the Massachusetts Statehouse in Boston and ultimately the White House, is still something of a presence in the Hampshire County city. Here he practiced law as part of the firm of Coolidge, Hemenway, Hemenway, and Graife. His two-hundred-dollar-a-year law office, upstairs in the Masonic Building at 25 Main Street above Fitzwilly's is as unassuming as the man himself. In fact, the door marked with the names of Coolidge and his law partners was removed a couple of years ago by the building's owner and given to Forbes Library, where it can be seen.

Coolidge, who reportedly continued to be briefed as president on probate cases weekly by a law partner who took a train to Washington, DC, moved after serving as president from a two-family house at 21 Massasoit Street. ("Nominate a man living in a two-family house? Never!" Henry Cabot Lodge told the 1920 Republican National Convention) to a thirteen-bedroom house, the Beeches on fifteen acres on Hampton Terrace. Both are private homes.

🏵 🏵 🏵

More obscure than Coolidge is Lydia Marie Child 1802-1880, who lived from May 1836 at an Elm Street boardinghouse on Northampton's Round Hill Road and moved near the site of what was to be the Pro Brush factory in Florence after a year, until 1841.

Medford-born Child, best known for her 1844 poem "Over the River and through the Woods," came to Northampton with her husband as part of his sugar beet research. She apparently disliked the city and left him to continue his research as she moved to New York to edit the *National Anti-Slavery Standard* and to champion women's rights.

An avid abolitionist, Child wrote several novels, including one she worked on in Northampton about the interracial marriage between a white settler and a Native American woman. Her other works included Afro-centered revisionist histories for the children of freed slaves and *The Frugal Housewife*, a popular domestic advice book. After abandoning popular novels, she concentrated on abolitionist works that are said to depict some of the more conservative people she had brushes with in Northampton.

A committee is now working on erecting a statue to Child, whom Amherst biographer David Dill called, "The best known female novelist of her time."

Compare with Smith College alum Julia Child, whose home on Francis Street in Cambridge is most likely the one with the aroma of sautéed onion, mushroom and je ne sais quoi with a bit of sherry, wafting out from the kitchen window at dinnertime. Then again, in the shadow of Harvard, it is a part of town known as Smart Street because it's home to economist John Kenneth Galbraith and other alleged intelligentsia. Gray smoke coming from the houses may be from all the brainstorming going on.

Northampton, where in 1844 Sojourner Truth first met Frederick Douglass and William Lloyd Garrison and gave her first speech as an abolitionist, was also the home of Sylvester Graham, the inventor of the Graham cracker and nineteenth-century temperance lecturer. Graham, whose home is now the site of the Pleasant Street restaurant that bears his first name, advocated vegetarianism, fresh foods, cold showers, lighter clothing, and coarsely ground whole wheat flour.

Related bakery item destinations may also include the former home of Kennedy Biscuits in Newton, originator of Fig Newtons, the state's official fruit cookie. The state's official non-fruit cookie is of course the Toll House cookie, named for the Toll House Restaurant in the Boston suburb of Wakefield.

Obviously, there are many more sites you can visit around the Bay State to suit your fancy. These are simply to whet your appetite for more.

photo by Richie Davis

A Sterling town common monument
acknowledges Mary's Little Lamb.

Acknowledgments

As I complete this trilogy of my favorite stories from four decades of reporting, I'm reminded of what a collaborative process it has been every step of the way and how blessed I am for the many creative people who have been so helpful and inspiring on my journey.

Writing is a solitary endeavor even in a busy newsroom. Yet the collaborative nature involved in interviewing subjects featured in this trilogy—often in intimate detail sharing the emotional range of their stories—is a primary. I feel privileged for the opportunity to be trusted by and allowed to empathize with them, and I'm deeply honored and grateful for that.

I'm very grateful to my editors at the Greenfield *Recorder* through the years, especially George Forcier, Don Pride, Tim Blagg, Neil Perry, Adam Orth, Denny Wilkins and Justin Abelson. I'm fortunate to have worked with so many talented reporters.

Appreciation to my editor and publisher Marcia Gagliardi for her encouragement and her attention to detail and for making this entire trilogy possible.

Thank you to photographer Paul Franz, who searched for many of his photographs that originally appeared with these stories. His careful eye has provided a window for the newspaper's readers for years. His work is at FranzPhoto.com

My appreciation to Greenfield *Recorder* Publisher Shawn Palmer for allowing me to share these stories anew.

Deep gratitude to my friend Ami Fagin, a very talented artist, for allowing her watercolor visual haiku, *First Signs of Spring*, to take flight on my cover. Her work is at visualhaiku.graphics.

Many thanks to my good friend, photographer Lindy Whiton, for her author's photo.

Thank you to Robin Locke Monda of Locke Monda Graphic Arts for her sensitivity in working with me on a cover design.

Profound love and appreciation to my wife, Susan Levine, for her insightful advice, her editing, and her help in so many ways.

A very special thank you to the people of Franklin County for making this region—originally the home of the Pocumtuck people—such a treasured place rich in moving stories and graceful beauty.

photo by Lindy Whiton

Richie Davis

About the Author

Richie Davis won more than thirty-five regional news and featurewriting awards as a reporter and editor for more than forty years at the *Recorder* of Greenfield in western Massachusetts. Engaging environmental, political, and societal issues, he wrote dozens of in-depth series on topics ranging from nuclear power and the aging population to high-tech cottage industries. He won a Pulitzer Center on Crisis Reporting grant for coverage of an effort to foster cross-cultural dialogue. But among his favorite works have been profiles of intriguing, ordinary people.

He blogs at his website, RichieDavis.net

Colophon

Text for *Flights of Fancy, Souls of Grace* is set in Adobe Garamond Pro, an Adobe Originals design and Adobe's first historical revival. Adobe Garamond is a digital interpretation of the roman types of Claude Garamond and the italic types of Robert Granjon. Since its release in 1989, Adobe Garamond has become a typographic staple throughout the world of desktop typography and design.

Titles and captions are set in Arial, a font designed for Monotype in 1982 by Robin Nicholas and Patricia Saunders. A contemporary sans serif design, Arial contains humanist characters.

Complete your set of stories from the Western Massachusetts heartland by Richie Davis

- a self-taught fiddler magically weaves community with his bow and heart
- a recovering substance abuser becomes chauffeur bodyguard and sometimes wrestling buddy for the Dalai Lama
- a tiny town adjusts to dozens of war refugees in its midst— "There was suspicion about who they were, why they were here, what kids they were going to snap up."
- an inner-city teen bonds with a 92-year-old farmer who's always lived off the land.
- a married couple reunites after five years of separation, ready to resume life together and renew vows as Sept. 11 attacks occur
- a lifelong polio victim, confined for decades of breathing-aid devices, soars by writing volumes of poetry.

Dig into these two story collections that open up a beneath-the-surface glimpse of extraordinary lives off the beaten path.

from Haley's * Athol, Masachusetts
Availalable online at RichieDavis.net

CPSIA information can be obtained
at www.ICGtesting.com
Printed in the USA
JSHW011218150723
44623JS00003B/10